BARNS & BACKBUILDINGS

**Designs for Barns, Carriage Houses, Stables, Garages & Sheds
with
Sources for Building Plans, Books, Timber Frames, Kits, Hardware, Cupolas & Weather Vanes**

Edited by Donald J. Berg, AIA

ISBN 0-9963075-0-X
Library of Congress
Catalog Card Number: 98-70418

Published by:
Donald J. Berg, AIA
P.O. Box 698
Rockville Centre, NY 11571-0698

Contents

Thanks

I'd like to thank everyone who contributed ideas, drawings, photos and designs. In particular, I'd like to thank Charles Leik, editor of the on-line magazine *The Barn Journal* (http://museum.cl.msu.edu/barn) for posting my queries. Dozens of his readers were kind enough to respond with information. David Stiles and Jerry Smith added their talent by preparing many of the drawings that you'll see. Jeanie Stiles, Lynn O'Connor, McKie Roth and Craig Wallin shared their knowledge of publishing. Jim Marks of *Joiners' Quarterly Magazine*, and timber framers Jeffrey Bradley, Ken Epworth, Ken Hume and Tom Musco sent material that helped me start to understand their craft. Lee Kogan of The Museum of American Folk Art helped with ideas on my research. I thank all of the folks at the museum for the use of their wonderful library.

My wife Christine improved the text with editing and ideas. My son Ted helped with barn website searches. I'd also like to thank them, my son Christopher and my daughter Bethany for being so patient with me. They took care of the rest of my life when I hid myself away in the attic to work on this.

Introduction

Barns & Backbuildings wasn't planned the way it turned out. Over the years I've done books on yesterday's buildings and landscaping. No one read them, but the old-time pictures were pretty. This was going to be another history picture book.

It happened that I was doing my research at the same as I noticed that the clutter around the yard at my family's country place was getting embarrassing. We needed a big shed or garage, at least for our neighbors' sake. I sat down at my drafting table to design something.

The two projects merged together. I put sliding doors, a loft and a loft hatch on my garage and had a little barn. It was practical, fun to draw, and it seemed just right for its Vermont site.

My friend, builder Bill Hardy, suggested that I look into pole-framing to save site work costs. I did, and I started to search for barn door hardware and a big lift post for the loft. What I found amazed me.

Barns aren't history.

There is a community of incredibly talented craftsmen, designers, authors and builders who make their livings working on barns. There are people who hand-forge beautiful iron strap hinges and others who design cupolas and whimsical weather vanes. There is a guild of professional framers, who practice the ancient craft of carving trees into post and beam frames. Some of them are preserving hundred year old heritage barns that have gotten in the way of progress. They carefully take apart the timbers or logs and rebuild them on new sites where they will serve for another few hundred years. There are new building guide books, historic associations and museums, magazines and great internet websites. Every architect, designer and builder seems to have a barn or two in the works, in the files, or at least in their thoughts.

I found that there was nothing that I would have told you about in a history book that isn't available, better, now. As I found new designs and resources, the history part shrunk from a book to just the few old-time illustrations that you'll see here and there. And, if you want barn history, you'll find some great books listed on the last few pages of this one.

If you're planning to build a barn, stable, garage, or shed you'll find designs, designers, and sources for specialty material. If you're restoring an old barn or carriage house, you'll find folks who can help as well as authentic hardware and supplies.

As I go to press with this, architects and designers are already putting together drawings for an expanded edition. I've probably overlooked many great manufacturers and artisans in the directory. I'll try to fix that before the next printing. In the meantime, I hope you enjoy your reading.

Don Berg, 2/28/98

These backbuildings look perfect together. You'd think that they were designed by the same hand. In fact, they are cobbled together from many of the different sources that you'll find in this book. They are here to show you how you can use *Barns & Backbuildings* to help create your own perfect country place.

The big stable is the 24' x 30' barn from John D. Wagner's book *Building a Multi-Use Barn*. You'll find information on that and many other useful building guides and references in Chapter 10. If you need fences and walls, you'll find some great books on how to build them yourself.

The cupola is a custom design by New England Cupola. The rooster weather vane is one of Denninger Weather Vanes' standard designs. You'll find many manufacturers of cupolas and weather vanes in Chapter 4, the Directory of Products and Services. There, you'll also find folks who hand-forge beautiful iron hinges and others who make barn doors and rolling door tracks. Looking for lightning rods and antique glass insulators? Look in the Directory.

The garage is a kit, just one of many designs from Country Carpenters, Inc. You'll find information on that company and other kit builders in the Directory. If you're looking for something different, how about an authentic old-time timber-framed building? You'll find artisans who have saved hundred year old barns to rebuild on your property and craftsmen who can build you a new timber frame for the next few hundred years.

The shed is a pole-frame design by architect Andy Sheldon. It's one of over ninety variations of designs by different architects and designers that you'll find in Chapters 5 through 8. They are all available as construction plans for your contractor. Some sheds and garden buildings are also available for your purchase as do-it-yourself drawings.

The buildings and details shown in the sketch on the last page represent the creations of eleven of the different designers and manufacturers included in this book. With so many designers, you'd think that result would be a hodgepodge. But, there are simple ways to make sure your buildings, old and new, will look great together. America's picture perfect farmsteads were created over years and years by different generations of builders. As you read through Chapters 2 and 3, you'll find out how they got great results using simple, traditional methods of site planning and design.

A custom stable design by Barns by Gardner, Ltd.
See the Directory of Products & Services for information.

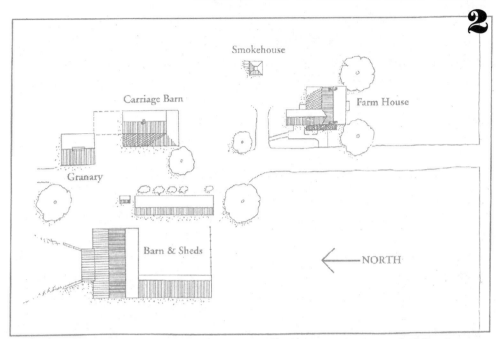

Farmstead Site Plan, drawn by William Macintire for the Historic American Building Survey

The old farmstead above is like thousands and thousands across America that share remarkably similar site plans. Even though the buildings were added over generations, they were built strictly on the square with each other. All walls are parallel or at right angles, even on buildings that are hundreds of yards away from one another. This gives a visual character that's a hallmark of American farm architecture. Old farmstead buildings seem as if they belong together, even if they are far apart, and even if they are very different in style, because they were carefully aligned with each other.

The visual effect is dramatic. Page through some of those great coffee-table books on barns and farms and you'll see. Drive through the countryside and you'll see it too. The places that catch your eye, that look just right and seem as if they have always been there and always will be, share the same simple method of site planning.

Keep it in mind as you plan your new backbuilding. A pretty barn, garage or shed, finished to complement your house, and aligned with it, can't fail to look great and improve the value of your property. And, it will cost you nothing more to plan your property right.

First, check on your community's zoning code. There may be setback distances between your property lines and where you are permitted to build. Make sure the area that you're planning to build on is clear of environmental or wetland restrictions. For secure foundations, you want to avoid marshy areas anyway. Have a surveyor, engineer or architect sketch a "building envelope," and show your existing buildings on the same plan. The information might already be on your survey. The envelope is the area that's clear of restrictions and that seems to have reasonably good soil.

Now, decide which building on your property is the most important or the most attractive. It's probably your home or a big barn. That's what your new backbuilding should be aligned with. Draw a rough outline of your new building at the same scale as your envelope plan. Cut it out and move it around the site plan. Remember to keep it aligned, on the square, with your house or barn. Imagine how it would look and work in different positions.

Make common sense decisions. A stable should be downhill from your well. The new carriage barn shouldn't block a nice view. Your new potting shed should be near the kitchen garden. Take your time. Walk around the area that you're thinking of and go through the same paces that you will with the new backbuilding. Drive your car or tractor into your imaginary garage. Make sure it can easily take the turns. Walk back to the house. How's that distance everyday?

If one best position doesn't win out, ask your architect, surveyor or engineer. It's always good to have an impartial opinion. They may see things that you didn't. That might make your decision easier.

Once you've picked a spot, you might need to present a site plan for zoning approval. Whoever plotted your building envelope can draw your new backbuilding on the same plan. Make sure that the new structure is aligned with the old ones and that dimensions are shown between the new and old buildings. That way it will be an easy job for your contractor to place the actual building in the right position in your yard.

If you build your new backbuilding well, it may stand there for the next few hundred years. Take the time now to make sure it's standing in the right spot. Plan it like the old timers did and, who knows, it might inspire a photo on some 22nd century coffee-table.

How to Find the Perfect Building
3

You should be able to use *Barns & Backbuildings* to find the perfect building for your needs. But first, you have to know exactly what you're looking for. How do you plan to use the building? Make a list of what it will hold. Set a budget. Imagine your new building sitting on the site you chose. How should it look against the other nearby buildings? Who will do the construction? Is this a do-it-yourself project or will you need an experienced contractor?

If you're new to it, the building process might seem complicated, but it really isn't. In this country, just about everyone builds. Barns, garages, stables and sheds are easy. You could even skip the careful planning. Most people do. But, you want the perfect building, so let's take it step by step.

Size

First, what size does your building have to be? How many vehicles will it park? How many stalls should it have? What equipment, supplies and tools do you have to store? If you have a boat, craft equipment, a farm tractor or a big truck, you'll need to take measurements. Find the overall width, length and height. You don't want to build a barn and then find that your tractor's roll over bar is too high for the door. It happens. Make sure to measure the full width of mowing decks and snow blowers on yard tractors and the length from the hitch of trailers.

Find out if your community has restrictions on building height or area. Many do. Check with your town or village office about its zoning codes. Most planned communities and subdivisions have their own restrictions. Find out code and community restrictions first and they won't be a worry. Many zoning codes look for the "apparent" height of a building instead of the actual height of the ridge. A building with a steeply pitched roof looks lower and is, on average, lower than a flat roofed building of the same overall height. Find the apparent height of your building by measuring to the lowest part of the main roof and then adding half the distance from that low point to the ridge. Cupolas and weather vanes can usually exceed the maximum height required by zoning codes.

Your Budget

Now set your budget. That's easy: you know what you can afford to pay. Remember that a well designed and well planned backbuilding will add value to your property. Do it right and that value will exceed what you pay. You can think of your new building as an investment and not just an expense.

Always have some funds in reserve. When you're building, expensive things go wrong with the weather. Inexpensive materials are always out of stock. And, there's always some costly finishing touch that you didn't plan on. That's just the nature of building. You can't avoid it, but you can plan on it. Always aim at spending ten or fifteen percent less than you can afford and keep the extra aside. Expect to use it on the unexpected.

If you're getting construction bids from different builders, have good sets of plans to give them. Make sure that each contractor is planning to provide the same materials and to take approximately the same amount of time. Ask the bidders to quote their price and the time it will take them to finish your job.

There are books written on how to find the best contractor. If you're concerned, it's worth a trip to your library. At the least, you should know that most professional builders are good at what they do and easy to work with, most backbuildings are fairly easy to build, and you'll do best working with a builder who has been recommended by people you trust. Call your town's building official, neighbors who have just built something, and local architects. Most will be glad to share their recommendations.

Don't just shop for price. Compare contractors' bids with their experience doing projects like yours. Avoid a contractor whose price is much higher than others and be wary of a price that's much lower. Most often that shows a miscalculation in the estimate. An honest mistake in calculation can put a builder in a financial bind. Most will honor their price and build grudgingly, but some will cut corners. You don't want either. The best bargain in building is a good contractor at a fair price.

It's best to control cost by choosing an efficient building design and selecting reasonably priced materials. In general, for the same size building, pole framing is the least expensive, followed by conventional light framing or stud construction. Timber framing is more expensive still and is usually reserved for showplace buildings. For sheds and small garden buildings factory-built units and kits are about the same price as site-built. If you have some experience materials alone, for a do-it-yourself project will cost about half what a contractor's job would.

Simple rectangular plans are usually the cheapest to build. Gable and shed roofs are less expensive than gambrels and hip roofs. Loft space is the cheapest storage you can build. It uses the same roof and foundation as the floor below and usually takes advantage of wasted volume in the shape of the roof. Traditional barn materials like vertical ship-lapped boards or boards and battens, zee-braced board doors and metal roofs tend to be the least expensive for the wear that they will take.

Most backbuildings can be financed by your bank. After they are built, their value becomes part of the value of your property. If you're planning to refinance your mortgage, you might consider waiting until after you build a new backbuilding to automatically include that new structure.

Cost, of course, shouldn't be the main criteria in your selection of a design. The type of backbuilding that improves the value of your place has to complement the look of your home and any other buildings you have. It has to look right for your neighborhood and for your yard.

There are a number of ways to make your new backbuilding or barn improve the appearance of your place. In the pages on planning your property, you read about orienting your new building "on the square" with your existing buildings. That's important. So is the color that you choose for the siding. Your paint or stain should match that of adjacent buildings. Siding on a barn, shed or stable can be different than what's on a house but siding on a garage, carriage house or any building close to the house should be the same. The new roof will also look best if it matches the old ones. Little details also help. Use the same hardware or decorative lamps or foundation stones around the place.

If you live in a pretty neighborhood, you'll want to help keep it that way. What makes it look good? If you live in a white house/red barn country village, enjoy that tradition and keep it. If you live by the sea where shingles are bleached silver by the salt air, shingle your barn and wait. Each region, each town, each neighborhood has a distinctive look born of years of climate and building tradition. That's a visual wealth and a value that you can easily add to your place. Find it and build a bit of it into your new building.

The actual style of your new building is probably less important than how it is placed on your property and how it's painted. Different gable roofs look good together. So do combinations of gables and shed roofs. Gambrel, hip and mansard roofs are so distinctive that it's difficult to cluster a few attractively. If your home or an existing barn has an unusual roof line, you'll probably do best with simple gable roofs on any new buildings.

Avoid stylish barns. Fashions change, but buildings remain. Look through some books on barns and old country buildings. You'll see hundred year old structures that still look great. That's what you should aim at. Ten years from now, when styles change, you'll be glad you did.

Framing Methods

The last thing that you have to consider in the choice of your building is the framing method, the way it will be built. You can invite your neighbors to join a barn raising bee for a traditional timber frame, or call your lumberyard and have a shed delivered.

Light Frame Construction

Most homes and residential buildings are built of wood stud walls and lightweight wood joists and roof rafters. You won't go wrong with light frame construction. Almost all contractors can do a good job of it, and modern materials like plywood sheathing, pressure treated sills and metal connectors almost guarantee a safe, long lasting structure. Most mail-order plans are for light frame buildings and most architects like to work with it. The cost is moderate.

Pole Framing

The second most popular building method, for today's barns and backuildings is pole framing. Large pressure treated posts are set into small footing holes and then the building structure is suspended off of them. Pole framing goes back to ancient aboriginal cultures, but it has only become popular again, recently. Modern preservatives protect the posts and give pole buildings long lives. Pole building can be substantially less expensive than conventional light frame construction because there is much less digging and site work to do, and much less concrete in the footings. Your should choose a contractor who has experience with pole buildings. A limited number of mail-order plans are available.

Timber Framing

The rarest building method today was once the most common. For the last hundred years, timber frame or "post and beam" construction was only widely used in Amish communities. Now, a growing number of artisans, called joiners, are working in the ancient craft. Huge timbers, sometimes most of the trunk of a tree, are cut with square edges and mortise and tendon joints. They are then shipped to the building site and assembled into large components, or bents, on the ground. A barn raising, by people power, or with the aid of a crane, lifts the bents into position and beams are inserted to connect them. The entire assembly is locked in place by wooden pegs. The frame stands like a skeleton until carpenters apply a roof, walls, doors and windows to turn it into a barn. And, what a barn! The thing will outlive your great grandchildrens' great grandchildren. It will look good inside and out and serve both as storage and sculpture. Building a timber frame is an adventure. You'll pay a fair premium over conventional construction, but you'll get what you pay for.

Heritage Barns

Another unusual way to a great building is to rebuild a heritage barn. A few joiners specialize in taking apart antique timber-frame or log barns and reassembling them to last for another few hundred years use. Because their inventory is usually made up of barns that are standing in the way of progress, you'll be preserving part of America's rural heritage when you rebuild one of these gems. The joiners will send you photos of their current selection of barns so that you can see if one suits your purpose. The prices are surprisingly reasonable for what you get. Remember that you're just buying the frame, so plan on additional cost for a new foundation and for closing the building in.

Kits and Prefabricated Buildings

You can also get a backbuilding for your property by purchasing a kit or prefabricated building. Factory building usually means top quality control. Sheds and small garden buildings can be shipped complete. You can use them the same day they are delivered to your yard. Other garden structures, larger sheds and small barns are shipped as pre-cut components. You or your builder have to put them together. A kit might be the answer if you want to do some of the work yourself but don't have power tools and don't enjoy trips to the lumber yard. With a pre-cut kit, you get to do just the fun part and still know that you built it yourself. Pre-cut kits are more expensive than materials alone, but for complicated small buildings like greenhouses and gazebos, they are often a bargain. The savings in wasted material and the value of good instructions are worth the extra cost.

How to Use This Book to Find Your Design

This book should get you started in the right direction toward finding your design. There are a number of chapters that will help.

Doing It Yourself, With Guide Books or Plans

If you are planning to build on your own, you'll find many designs and how-to information in the books in Chapter 10. Even if you're planning to have a professional do the work, knowing about the construction process can help you enjoy it more. A few of the garden building designs in Chapter 8 make great do-it-yourself projects. Clear construction plans are available from their designers.

The Directory

Chapter 4 is the Directory of Products and Services. Page through it to find kit manufacturers, builders, joiners, designers and heritage timber frames.

Mail-Order Building Designs

In Chapters 5 through 8, you'll find more than ninety variations of designs for all types of barns and backbuildings. Most are conventional light frame buildings, but you'll also find some timber frames and pole buildings. Construction drawings are available for all, directly from their designers. Many of the designers will modify the drawings to your exact needs.

Custom Designs

If you can't find any design that suits you, you'll need a custom design. Ask builders and your town's building officials to recommend architects. Contact your state's chapter of the American Institute of Architects for a list of members in your area. Most state chapters are located in the capital city.

Speak with a few architects and try to find someone who you'll enjoy working with and who seems enthusiastic about your project. An architect will spend time with you to find your needs and then more time creating and presenting designs to you and preparing contract documents. The service can include help with the bidding process and site inspections during construction. Prices vary, but you should expect to pay from 10% to 15% of the total construction cost of your building for full architectural services on a great one-of-a-kind building.

How to Use the Designs Chapters

The pages of backbuilding designs in Chapters 5 through 8 have been set up to help make your search easy.

Floor Plans

All of the floor plans in this book are drawn at the consistent scale of 1/16" =1'-0". You can quickly compare the size of the designs from one page to the next. You can also see if your truck, trailer or equipment will fit in a building. Measure your equipment or vehicles and then draw them to scale. Draw each foot in length or width as 1/16" of an inch - the smallest unit between lines on most rulers. Now, cut out the plan you made and drop it on one of the building plans. If the plan of your truck or tractor fits in the plan on the page, you'll know that it will fit into that barn. Make sure that you leave yourself room to open doors and walk around.

Building Statistics

The most vital information is printed at the upper corner of each page. That includes the overall size of the building, its actual height, its apparent height for your zoning department, the type of construction that it was designed for, and a range of probable building costs.

Cost Estimates

It's impossible to accurately estimate what your building cost will be. Prices vary with your location, with the conditions of your site, with the season that you build in and with the materials and finishes that you choose. The range shown is wide enough to include most, but not all of the possible variables. It is estimated as work by a professional builder. Materials alone should be about half the cost listed.

Since all of the ranges were estimated using the same standards, they work best as a way to compare different designs. A design that's less expensive than another in this book will also be less expensive on your site.

Acorn Forged Iron

457 School Street, P.O. Box 31, Mansfield, MA 02048
Decorative builders' hardware for exterior and interior doors, cabinets, gates and shutters. Catalog: $10.00. Free product literature. Phone 800 835-0121. Fax 800 372-2676. Website: www.acornmfg.com
New Forged Hardware

Allen Cupolas

2242 Bethel Road, Lansdale, PA 19446
Allen Cupolas has a complete selection of cupolas in poplar, redwood and cedar, with copper, brass or aluminum roofs. Custom sawmill capabilities on premises. Free brochure. Phone 610 584-8100 or phone, then Fax 215 699-8100. E-mail: vickallen@msn
Cupolas, Woodwork

Antique Hardware & Home

19 Buckingham Plantation Dr., Bluffton, SC 29901
Replica hardware and accessories (many found nowhere else). 300 styles of door and cabinet hardware, weathervanes, tin ceilings, and cast iron barn bells, boot scrapers and horse hitches. Phone 800 422-9982. Fax 803 837-9789. E-Mail: treasure@hargray.com
Antique Hardware, New Hardware, Cupolas, Weathervanes

Architectural Antiques Exchange

715 North 2nd Street, Philadelphia, PA 19123
Architectural salvage including doors, street lamps, leaded and beveled glass, signs, paneling and much more. Free catalog. Phone 215 922-3669. Fax 215 922-3680
Architectural Salvage

Allen Cupolas

Architectural Iron Company - Capital Cresting

P.O. Box 126, Milford, PA 18337
America's leading producer of roof cresting offers a complete line of lightweight, easy to install, economical to ship, unbreakable steel roof cresting, matching finials and snowguards. Custom sizes are available. Free Catalog. Phone 800 442-IRON. Fax 717 296-IRON
Finials, Cresting, Snowguards

Acorn Forged Iron

The Barn People

P.O. Box 4, Morgan Hill, South Woodstock, VT 05071-0004
Offering a standing inventory of antique New England barn frames which can be dismantled, restored and reassembled anywhere in the United States. Free literature. Phone 802 457-3356. Fax 802 457 3358. E-Mail: barnman@souer.net
Heritage Timber Frames, Custom Design

Barns by Gardner, Ltd.

3833 West County Road 8, Berthoud, CO 80513
Custom design and building of pole barns and stables in northern Colorado. From simple loafing sheds to elegant showplace stables, Steve Gardner and his crew will build to the highest standards of quality, with the best materials, and at reasonable prices. Free literature. Phone 970 532-3595
Custom Barn and Stable Design & Building, Building Plans

Donald J. Berg, AIA

P.O. Box 698, Rockville Centre, NY 11571-0698
Member of the American Institute of Architects and the Society of Architectural Historians and author or editor of books on American country buildings, like this one. See the *Carriage Barn & Garage Designs* and *References* sections for samples. Custom design of new country buildings, historic research and renovations of old ones. Phone 516 766-5585
Custom Design, Historic Renovations, Building Plans

Belcher's

2505 West Hillview Drive, Dalton, GA 30721
Pre-Civil War log cabins, weathered barn siding, split rails, hand-hewn beams. Consulting on restoration of old log cabins. Free literature. Phone 706 259-3482
Architectural Salvage, Restoration Services

Bessler Stairway Company

3807 Lamar Ave., Memphis, TN 38118
A bessler one-piece sliding stairway is an excellent choice for loft and attic access. Free catalog. Phone 901 360-1900. Fax 901 795-1253. E-Mail: bessler@bessler.com
Website: www.bessler.com
Pull-down Stairs

Big Springs Preservation Group, Inc.

1004 West Summer Street, Greenville, TN 37743
Dismantling, restoration and reassembly of antique log cabins, barns, outbuildings, garden sheds, and timber frame barns and houses. Free product literature. Phone 423 787-9373 Fax 423 787-9374
Heritage Timber Frames, Restoration Services, Garden Structures, Antique Cabins & Outbuildings

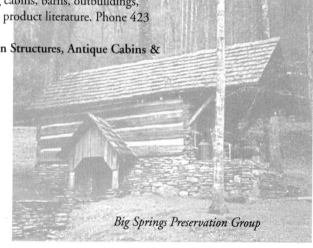

Big Springs Preservation Group

Board & Beam Co.

60 Wykeham Road, Washington, CT 06793

Dismantled barns and salvaged materials including beams, planks, doors, hardware and architectural details. Sells entire buildings for reconstruction. Phone 860 868-6789. Fax 860 868-0721. E-mail: bbeams@ct1.nai.net

Heritage Timber Frames, Salvaged Lumber, Woodwork Details and Barn Doors, Antique Hardware

Bouvet USA, Inc.

540 Dettaro Street, San Francisco, CA 94107

Decorative hardware company, established in 1884, offers a wide selection of hand forged iron hardware. The products are made in France and adapted to US standards. Phone 415 864-0273. Fax 800-ATBOUVET. E-Mail: info@bouvet.com

Antique and Custom Hardware

Bow House/Bow Bends

P.O Box 900, Bolton, MA 01740

Makers of fine quality traditional cottages and garages plus exotic garden structures: bridges, gazebos, arbors, follies, privies, and trellage. Catalog: $5.00. Phone 978 779-6464. Fax 978 779-2272

Garden Structures, Building Kits

Brandywine Valley Forge

P.O. Box 1129, Valley Forge, PA 19481-9998

Restoration blacksmiths specializing in hand forged hardware - strap hinges & pintles, hooks & hasps, barn door and gate bolts. Custom work done. Catalog; $5.00 or send a self-addressed stamped envelope for free literature. Phone 610 948-5116. Fax 610 933-4305

Hand Forged Hardware

Brosamer's Bells

207 Irwin Street, Brooklyn, MI 49230

Bells for barn yards, backyards, cupolas, etc. Brass, cast iron & bronze, antique and new. Brosamer's it the country's largest dealer of pre-owned bells. Free product literature. Phone 517 592-9030. Fax 517 592-4511

Barn and Yard Bells

Architectural Iron/Capital Cresting

Branywine Valley Forge

The Barn People

Cannonball: HNP

555 Lawton Ave., Beloit, WI 53512

Cannonball: HNP is an 81 year old company that produces sliding door systems, tracks, trolleys, windows, walk doors, dutch doors, horse stalls, foil insulation, ventilators and cupolas for the agricultural marketplace. Free catalog. Phone 608 365-2161

Doors, Windows, Hardware and Specialties for Barns, Stables and Agricultural Buildings

Cape Cod Cupola Co., Inc.

78 State Road, North Dartmouth, MA 02747

Cape Cod Cupola Company manufactures cupolas and weathervanes and specializes in custom work for both. Largest selection of cupolas, weathervanes, sundials & house signs. Catalog: $2.00, refundable with first order. Phone 508 994-2119. Fax 508 997-2511

Cupolas, Weathervanes

Chestnut Oak Co.

3810 Old Mountain Road, West Suffield, CT 06093-2125

Chestnut Oak Co. specializes in historic preservation. They dismantle, move and erect old timber-framed homes and barns throughout the Northeast. They also create new custom timber-frame buildings as you'll see in the *Barn Designs* section of this book. Product literature is free. Phone 860 668-0382. Fax 860 668-0382

Heritage Timber Frames, New Timber Frames

CinderWhit & Company

733 Eleventh Avenue South, Wahpeton, ND 58075

Stock, replica or custom turnings, including porch posts, finials, newel posts, balusters and spindles for exterior and interior applications. Free brochure. Phone 800 527-9064. Fax 701 642-4204

Wood Turnings

Colonial Cupolas, Inc.

1816 Nemoke Trail, P.O. Box 38, Haslett, MI 48840

America's largest selection of cupolas, assembled or as kits. Catalog: $3.00. Product Literature: $3.00. Phone 517 349-6185

Cupolas, Weathervanes, Sundials, Cast Metal Date & Street Number Plaques

Coppercraft, Inc.

2143 Joe Field Road, Suite 100, Dallas, TX 75229

Coppercraft utilizes traditional metalworking skills and modern technology to create high quality architectural sheet metal products including cupolas, spires, weathervanes and more. Free catalog and product literature. Phone 800 486-2723. Fax 972 484-3008. E-Mail: info@coppercraft.com Website: www.coppercraft.com

Cupolas, Finals, Spires, Gutters, Vents, Roofing

The Copper House

1747 Dover Road (Route 4), Epsom, NH 03234-4416

Brass & copper interior and exterior lighting; copper weathervanes. All products made in New Hampshire. Lighting is U.L. approved. Catalog: $4.00. Phone 800 281-9798. Fax 603 736-9798. Website: www.northwindnh.com/copper

Post Lamps, Carriage House Lamps, Weathervanes

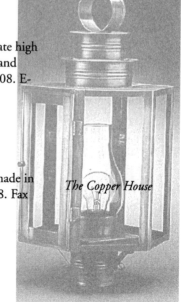

The Copper House

Country Carpenters, Inc.
5 Webster Lane, Boulton CT 06043
Designers and manufacturers of fine pre-cut, New England style post & beam barns, carriage houses, garages & sheds. Catalog: $4.00. Phone 860 649-0822. Fax 860 645-7678. Website: www.countrycarpenters.com
Building Kits

Craftwright Incorporated
100 Railroad Ave., Suite 105, Westminister, MD 21157
Custom, handcrafted timber frames. Antique timbers and frames available. Phone 410 876-0999
Heritage Timber Frames, New Timber Frames

Crosswinds Gallery, Inc.
29 Buttonwood Street, Bristol, RI 02809
Large selection of quality weathervanes, cupolas and finials in a variety of materials and at a variety of prices. Crosswinds Gallery specializes in custom design and crafting. Imagine a weathervane and they'll make it for you. Extensive catalog of designs is free. Phone 401 253-0334. Fax 401 253-2830. E-mail: wvanes@aol.com. Website: www.crosswinds.gallery.com
Weathervanes, Finials, Cupolas, Custom Design

Cumberland General Store
#1 Highway 68, Crossville, TN 38555
General merchandise catalog with old-time and country specialties and restoration & building products. Weathervanes, boot scrapers, hitching posts, farm bells, farmstead tools, hardware, country home plans, pumps, windmills and building books. Catalog: $4.00. Phone 931 484-8481. Fax 931 456-1211. E-mail: generalstore@worldnet.att.net Website: www.cumberlandgeneral.com
Hardware, Books, Building Plans, Weathervanes

Cumberland Woodcraft Company
P.O. Drawer 609, 10 Stover Drive, Carlisle, PA 17013
Interior and exterior Victorian millwork, gables, balustrades, corbels and brackets, mouldings and custom items. Catalog: $5.00. Phone 800 367-1884. Fax 717 243-6502. E-Mail: cwc@pa.net Website: www.pa.net/cwc/
Woodwork, Finials & Cresting

Dad's Woodshop
19392 Renwood Ave., Euclid, OH 44119
Dad's is a full service custom woodshop focusing on specialty and hard to find products. Product literature: $1.00. Phone 216 383-8808
Woodwork, Cupolas, Arbors, Trellises

Country Carpenters

Dalton Pavilions, Inc.

20 Commerce Drive, Telford, PA 18969
Dalton Pavilions Inc. offers fine western red cedar prefabricated pavilions and garden structures that can be shipped throughout the U.S. and internationally. Free catalog. Phone 215 721-1492. Fax 215 721-1501
Prefabricated Garden Structures

Denninger Weather Vanes & Finials

77 B Whipple Road, Middletown, NY 10940
Finely handcrafted horses, roosters, eagles, banners, scrolls, arrows, caps and finials. Custom and standard designs. Farm and business logos. Historic replications. Informative website for anyone interested in the art and lore of weather vanes. Free literature. Phone 914 342-2229. Fax 914 343-2229. E-Mail: al@denninger.com Website: www.denninger.com
Weathervanes, Finials

Eagle Creek Designs, Inc.

6025 Schustrich Road, P.O. Box 163, Mantua, OH 44255
Eagle Creek Designs stocks log houses, timber frames, cut sandstone, ornamental stone, mantles, flooring, hardware, beadboard and beams. Phone 330 274-2041 for more information.
Building Materials, Heritage Timber Frames

English Barns to America

P.O. Box 580, Walpole, NH 03608
Specialist in salvaging and importing English barns. Free literature. Phone or Fax: 603 756-3434
Heritage Timber Frames

Eugenia's Antique Hardware

5370 Peachtree Road, Chamblee, GA 30341
Authentic antique hardware - no reproductions. Door and furniture hardware, hinges, handles, latches, knockers, mechanical bells & forged iron strap hinges. Catalog: $1.00. Phone 800 337-1677. Fax 770 458-5966
Antique Hardware

Fingerlakes Weathervanes and Cupolas

P.O. Box 554, Canandaigua, NY 14424
Unique copper and brass weathervanes, made in the U.S.A. Combination brass and copper American flag weathervanes for $300.00. Free Catalog and product literature. Phone 716 394-1091
Weathervanes, Finials & Cresting

Fingerlakes Westhervanes & Cupolas

Garden Oak Specialties

1921 Route 22 West, Bound Brook, NJ 08805
Manufacturers of high quality, prefab garden buildings including sheds, gazebos, arbors, playhouses and mailboxes in a variety of stiles. Buildings are shipped complete to your backyard. Free literature. Phone 800 590-7433. Fax 732 356-7202. E-mail: info@gardenoaks.com   Website: www.gardenoaks.com
Prefabricated Sheds and Garden Buildings

Glass House

50 Swedetown Road, Pomfret Center, CT 06259
Glass House is a custom fabricator of richly profiled wood frame conservatories in various shapes - hip, gable and lantern roofs and octagons. Glass house also makes pyramidal skylights.
Free catalog. Phone 800 222-3065. Fax 860 974-1173
Garden Structures, Conservatories, Skylights

Great Northern Barns

Box 912E, RFD 2, Canaan, NH 03741
Great Northern Barns works with all aspects of timber framing with an emphasis on selling and erecting antique barn frames. Free literature. Video: $10.00. Phone 603 523-7134. Fax 603 523-7134. Website: www.greatnorthernbarns.com
Heritage Timber Frames

Gothic Arch Greenhouses

P.O. Box 1564-BB, Mobile, AL 36633
Gothic Arch Greenhouses, a division of Trans-Sphere Trading Corp., creates beautiful Gothic style greenhouse kits in redwood, with polycarbonate glazing, in hobby and backyard to commercial sizes. Designs are free standing or lean-to. They also provide heating, cooling, ventilation and humidification systems for greenhouses. Product literature: $2.00. Phone 334 432-7529. Fax 334 432-7972
Greenhouse Kits and Environmental Systems

Green Star Forge

3 Myrtle Street, Taunton, MA 02780-4111
One-man shop specializing in custom forged iron work. Catalog: $2.00. Phone 508 824-3077
Hand Forged Iron Hardware

Denninger Weather Vanes & Finials

Hahn Woodworking Company

Hager Companies

139 Victor Street, St.Louis, MO 63104
Manufacturer of hinges and builders' hardware including barn door rollers, tracks and accessories, strap hinges, shed hardware, metal thresholds, door sweeps and gate hardware. Free catalog and product literature. Phone 314 772-4400. Fax 314 772-0744
Hardware, Barn Door Rollers & Track

Hahn Woodworking Company, Inc.

109 Aldene Road, Roselle, NJ 07203
Custom wooden garage doors built to your specifications: stile and rail doors with flat or raised panels; historic barn and carriage-house style doors with convenient overhead motorized operation; traditional swing-out and sliding doors. Free catalog and product literature. Phone 908 241-8825. Fax 908 241-9293
Barn & Garage Doors, Custom Design

William T. Hardy, Builder

Rural Route 2, Box 344, North Bennington VT 05257
Fine craftsmanship of barns and country homes. Custom builds in pole-framing, light-frame and log construction in southern Vermont, northwestern Massachusetts and eastern New York. Pole-frame consultant to *Barns & Backbuildings*. Phone 802 442-4075
Custom Builder

Heritage Restoration

122 South Church Avenue, Bozeman, MT 59715
Historical design and construction consulting, specializing in old houses and period designs. New carriage houses designed to compliment historic homes. Free literature. Phone 406 587-8082
Restoration Services, Custom Design

Historic Housefitters Co.

P.O. Box 26, 32 Centre, Route 312, Brewster, NY 10509
Hand forged iron hardware of all types. Strap hinges and pintles, cane bolts, thumb latches, door pulls. Stock hardware, custom designs and reproductions. Catalog: $3.00. Phone 914 278-2427. Fax 914 278-7726
New Hardware, Custom Reproductions

Hager Companies

Gothic Arch Greenhouses

Holmes Garage Door

P.O. Box 1976, Auburn, WA 98071-1976
Holmes Garage Door manufactures a complete line of custom, hand crafted wood garage doors. The "Carriage House" door is a wood roll-down that simulates historic swinging doors. Free product literature. Phone 253 931-8900. Fax 253-939-8508
Barn & Garage Doors

Homestead Design, Inc.

P.O. Box 2010, Port Townsend, WA 98368
You'll find many of Homestead Design's barns, stables, garages and sheds in the *Designs* pages of this book. The buildings feature flexible plans and simple framing. Mail-order plans are easy to understand, easy to use, and include a list of the materials you'll need to build the structure and exterior shell. Interior finishes and a variety of interior layouts are your choice. You can build these designs just the way you want. Catalog: $3.00. Phone 360 385-9983
Building Plans

Ken Hume, Engineer

Oakhurst, Sherfield Road, Bramley, Hampshire, England RG26 5AQ
Registered professional engineer practicing in the USA and UK. Timber-frame designer and structural analyst with an understanding of traditional practices in America and Europe. Phone 011 44 1256 881344. E-mail: ken.hume@pareuro.com
Timber Frame Engineering, Restoration Services

Independent Protection Co., Inc.

1603-09 South Main Street, P.O. Box 537, Goshen, IN 46527
Ornamental and conventional lightning protection equipment, systems and products for all types of barns and related structures. Catalog: $10.00. Product Literature: $5.00. Phone 219 533-4116. Fax 219 534-3719. E-Mail: ipc@netbahn.net
Lightning Rods, Weathervanes

Iron Intentions Forge

RD#2 Box 2399C, Spring Grove, PA 17362
Custom forged hardware and accents in steel, stainless, brass, copper and aluminum. Phone 717 229-2665
Antique Hardware, New Hardware, Weathervanes

Heritage Restoration

William T. Hardy, Builder

Ives Weathervanes

Box 101A, RR1, Charlemont, MA 01339
Hand formed, elegant custom copper and brass weathervanes. Three dimensional hammer formed with "chased" in details, or two dimensional silhouette styles. Gold leafing available. Catalog: $1.00. Phone 413 339-8534
Weathervanes

Jack's Country Store

P.O. Box 710, Bay Avenue & Highway 103, Ocean Park, WA 98640
Jack's genuine Alladin kerosene lamps are smokeless, odorless and as bright as a 60-watt light bulb. Great for non-electric outbuildings. Complete selection of lamps and parts. Catalog: $1.00. Phone 360 665-4988. Fax 360 665-4989
Kerosene Lamps, Hardware

Just Outbuildings

P.O. Box 42, Brewster, NY 10509
Just Outbuildings produces complete building plans for garages, sheds, poolhouses and garden buildings in a variety of sizes. Styles range from contemporary to traditional. Plans can be customized to suit your needs. See samples of Just Outbuildings' creations on the *Designs* pages of this book. Catalog: $6.00. Phone 914 279-4542. E-Mail: gjgaspar@bestweb.net
Building Plans, Custom Design

Kayne & Son Custom Hardware, Inc.

100 Daniel Ridge Road, Chandler, NC 28715
Custom forged hardware, strap hinges, latches, bolts, braces, door rollers, hasps, locks, branding irons, restoration, repairs and reproduction of antique hardware. Catalog: $5.00. Phone 704 667-8868. Fax 704 665-8303. E-Mail: kaynehdwe@ioa.com
New Forged Hardware, Restoration Services

Kolter Farms

Route 83, Ellington, CT 06029
Kolter farms offers excellent value on storage buildings, gazebos, lawn furniture and cupolas. Customer satisfaction guaranteed since 1980. Free Catalog and product literature. Phone 800 289-3463. Fax 860 871-1117. E-Mail: sales@kolterfarms.com. Website: www.kolterfarms.com
Building Kits, Garden Structures, Prefabricated Buildings, Cupolas, Weathervanes

Holmes Garage Door

Ives Weathervanes

Landmark Services, Inc.

Landmark Services, Inc. is a restoration and renovation general contracting firm with a skilled crew of carpenters, masons and painters. Barns Restored, repaired, disassembled and reassembled. Free literature. Phone or Fax 508 533-8393. E-Mail: LndmarkSer@aol.com

Restoration Services

Lehman's

One Lehman Circle, P.O. Box 41, Kidron, OH 44636
Lehman's 160 page non-electric catalog contains 2,500 items you thought weren't made any more, including farm tools, wood stoves, grain mills, butter churns, copper kettles and more. Catalog: $3.00. Phone 330 857-5757. Fax 330 857-5785. E-Mail: info@lehmans.com

Hardware, How-to Books, Tools, Gas Lamps

Lemee's Fireplace Equipment.

815 Bedford Street, Bridgewater, MA 02324
Wrought iron hardware, strap hinges, boot scrapers, barn bells and gongs, hitching posts, weathervanes. Catalog: $2.00. Phone 508 697-2672

Antique Hardware, New Hardware, Weathervanes

Lester Building Systems

1111 2nd Avenue South, Lester Prairie, MN 55354
Lester Building Systems, a division of Butler Manufacturing Company, manufactures pre-engineered wood frame structures for agricultural, equestrian, commercial and suburban use. Product literature is available. Phone 800 826-4439. Fax 320 395-2969. E-Mail: marketing@lesterbuildingsystems.com Website: www.lesterbuildingsystems.com

Pre-engineered Post Frame Buildings, Custom Design

Linear Rubber Products

5525 19th Avenue, Kenosha, WI 53140
Manufacturer of "Soft Stall" stable mats which are nonabsorbent, and easy to install. These resilient mats will help keep your horse healthy while cutting cost and labor of stable upkeep. Free catalog and product literature. Phone 800 558-4040. Fax 414 657-6705

Stable Mats

The Mailbox Shoppe

2566A Hempstead Turnpike, East Meadow, NY 11554
The Mailbox Shoppe represents over 30 manufacturers of weathervanes, cupolas, mailboxes, mailbox posts, custom cast signs and other home accessories. Free catalog and product literature. Phone 800 330-3309. Fax 516 735-6191. E-mail: sales@mailboxnet.com Website: www.mailboxnet.com

Mailboxes, Cupolas, Weathervanes

The Mailbox Source

12367 Deerbrook Lane, Los Angeles, CA 90049-1909
Residential freestanding and wall-mounted mailboxes in a wide variety of styles and materials: locking boxes; large capacity boxes; novelty boxes. Free catalog. Phone or Fax 800 209-0111

Mailboxes

Independent Protection Company

Lemee's Fireplace Equipment

The Millworks, Inc.

P.O. Box 2987, Durango, CO 81302
Victorian, Traditional, Country and Southwest millwork. Catalog: $2.00. Phone 970 259-5915. Fax 970 259-5919
Woodwork

New England Cupola

184 Mattapoisett Road, Acushnet, MA 02743
Builder of fine, hand crafted cupolas in a wide range of styles and sizes. Custom work is New England Cupola's specialty. Free catalog and product literature. Phone 508 995-5331. Fax 508 998-7041
Cupolas, Weathervanes, Custom Design

New England Outbuildings

P.O. Box 621, Westbrook, CT 06498
New England Outbuildings creates new farm and garden outbuildings in the traditional manner by meticulously preserving the lines, proportion and details of New England's historic buildings. Post & beam frames are milled from oak, cut with mortise & tendon joints and shipped to your site, to be assembled with wooden pegs. Frame kits include designs for barns, wagon sheds, corn cribs and more. Free literature. Phone 860 669-1776
New Timber Frames, Building Kits

New Jersey Barn Company

P.O. Box 702, Princeton, NJ 08542
New Jersey Barn Company offers antique oak barn timber frames which they re-erect on your property. Free literature. Phone 609 924-8480. Fax 609 730-1030
Heritage Timber Frames

North Woods Joinery

P.O. Box 1166, Burlington, VT 05402-1166
Traditional post & beam structures - gazebos, barns, sheds, homes and more. Choice of wood species includes pine, hemlock, oak and Douglas fir. See the *Barn Designs* section of this book for a sample of North Woods' creations. Free product literature. Phone 802 644-2400 or 802 644-2500. Fax 802 644-2509
New Timber Frames, Building Kits

New Jersey Barn Company

Russell Swinton Oatman Design Associates, Inc.

132 Mirick Road, Princeton, MA 01541

Where the past is present. Authentic reproductions of traditional home exteriors with modern interior layouts and careful attention to details. Portfolios include: the Old Sturbridge Village Collection, $7.00; the New England Collection, $8.00; the Victorian Collection, $8.00; and the Cape Cod Collection, $8.00. Construction plans are available for all designs and all can be customized to your needs. See the *Designs* pages of this book for samples of architect Russell Swinton Oatman's buildings. Phone 978 464-2360

Building Plans, Custom Design

O'Brock Windmills

9435 12th Street, North Benton, OH 44449

O'Brock Windmills sells and installs old style water pumping windmills which are very often found next to old barns. They were, and still are, used to provide water for livestock. Today, many people install them just to look good turning in the breeze. Catalog: $2.00. Phone 330 584-4681. Fax 330 584-4682. E-Mail: windmill@cannet.com

Water Pumping Windmills, Hand Pumps, Hydraulic Rams

The Painted Garden

304 Edge Hill Road, Glenside, PA 19038

Handcrafted iron garden structures: arbors, trellises, archways, gates, pavilions, benches and pergolas in the tradition of elegance, beauty and permanence. Catalog: $3.00. Phone 215 884-7378

Garden Structures, Custom Design

Recycled Products Company

18294 Amber Road X44, Monticello, IA 52310-7708

Manufacturer of plastic lumber and "100 Year" barn windows, recycled from milk containers. White, venting barn windows are USDA approved, never need paint or putty, come in a variety of efficient, attractive sizes and help reduce landfill waste. Free product literature. Phone 800 765-1489. Fax 319 465-1489

Barn Sash and Windows, Recycled Lumber

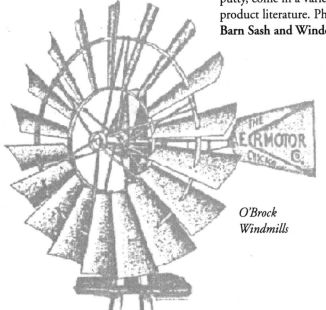

O'Brock Windmills

New England Cupola

Ritchie Industries, Inc.

120 South Main, P.O. Box 730, Conrad, IA 50621
Ritchie offers a full line of automatic livestock fountains for all types and sizes of operation. Choose from steel or polyethylene construction and heated or electric-free.
Livestock Waterers

McKie Roth Design, Inc.

P.O. Box 31, Castine, ME 04421
You'll find some of McKie Wing Roth's barns in the *Designs* sections of this book, but he is best known for his exquisite traditional New England home designs. His folio of home designs features thirty five Capes, Colonials, Saltboxes and Gambrels, all with contemporary interior layouts for modern living, and all with construction plans you can order. The folio features study plans and articles on capturing the old look, exterior colors, preserving finishes and the advantages of good proportion and details to achieve a timeless character. Catalog: $18.00. Phone 800 232-7684. Fax 207 326-9513
Building Plans, Traditional Home and Barn Designs

Royalston Oak Timber Frame

122 North Fitzwilliam Road, Royalston, MA 01331
New England and medieval English timber frames in oak, pine, hemlock and fir. Traditional wooden joinery with the highest quality timbers. See Royalston Oak's recreation of an 18th century New England barn in the *Barn Designs* section of this book. Catalog: $8.00. Free literature. Phone 800 317-1129. Fax 978 249-9633
New Timber Frames, Medieval English-Style Timber Frames

Salter Industries

P.O. Box 183, Eagleville, PA 19408
Steel and wood spiral stairs in a variety of sizes and designs including half-turns and units that meet BOCA and UBC code requirements. Free literature. Phone 610 631-1306. Fax 610 631-9384
Spiral Stairs

A.F. Schwerd Manufacturing Co.

3215 McClure Avenue, Pittsburgh, PA 15212
Standard and custom wood columns, pilasters and ornamental capitals. Optional aluminum bases for exterior columns. In business since 1860. A.F. Schwerd can match your existing columns. Free product literature. Phone 412 766-6322. Fax 412 766-2262
Wood Columns, Turned Wood Posts

Second Harvest Salvage

RR#1, Box 194E, Jeffersonville, VT 05464
Antique hand-hewn barn and house frames, wide board flooring, kits available. Call Second Harvest Salvage and save a tree. Phone 802 644-8169
Heritage Timber Frames, Restoration Services

The Painted Garden

David Shea

48 Center Street - Route 322, Wolcott, CT 06716

Dave Shea has an inventory of approximately 50 antique horse-drawn vehicles for sale for commercial or pleasure use, or for collectors. Wagons, carriages, carts and sleds range from draft horse to pony sizes. Antique stable appointments are also available. For information, phone 203 879-3169

Antique Horse Drawn Vehicles, Stable Equipment

Sheldon Designs, Inc.

1330 Route 206 - #204, Skillman, NJ 08558

Besides the great barns, stables, garages and sheds that you can see in the *Designs* section of this book, architect Andy Sheldon has created a line of country cabins and cottages from one room wilderness getaways to elegant shingle-style vacation homes. Detailed building plans are available for all. Many can also be purchased as pre-cut, easy-to-build log kits. Catalog: $6.00. Phone 800 572-5934. Fax 609 683 5976

Building Plans, Custom Design, Building Kits

Spiral Stairs of America, Inc.

1700 Spiral Court, Erie, PA 16510-1367

Spiral, curved and straight stair systems for in and out door use. Made of steel, wood or aluminum. Free product literature. Phone 800 422-3700. Fax 814-899-9139

Stairs

Stiles Designs

4 Albertine Lane. East Hampton, NY 11937

Besides writing best selling books like *Sheds, Storage Projects You Can Build, Rustic Retreats,* and the new *Tree Houses You Can Actually Build.* Jeanie and David Stiles have do-it-yourself plans for garden structures, play houses and home storage projects. All of the plans are clearly illustrated and guide you, step by step, to great results. You'll see some of the Stiles'creations in the *Shed & Garden Building Designs* section of this book. Product literature: $5.00. Phone or Fax 212 427-2317. E-Mail: jeandave@AOL.com

Designs for Sheds, Playhouses and Garden Structures, Do-It-Yourself Plans

Sunbuilt Solar Products by Sussman, Inc.

109-10 180th Street, Jamacia, NY 11433

Prefabricated glass and aluminum sunrooms available in curved or straight eave design. Modular design. Kneewall, glass-to-ground, extra high and two story configurations are available. Free catalog and product literature. Phone 718 297-6040. Fax 718 297-3090

Prefabricated Sunrooms

Timber Creek Post and Beam Inc.

P.O. Box 309, Cuttingsville, VT 05738

Timber-framed barns and homes, handcrafted from eastern white pine. Custom design, quality and flexibility are part of Timber Creek's tradition. Free literature. Phone 802 492-3932. Fax 802 775-6591

New Timber Frames, Custom Design

Weather or Knot Antiques

8504 West 1350 S, P.O. Box 321, Wanatah, IN 46390

Lightning rod glass ornaments, modern and antique. Antique rods and weathervanes. Restoration material for lightning protection memorabilia. Catalog: $10.00. Phone 219 733-2530

Lightning Rods, Decorative Glass Insulators, Weathervanes

West Coast Weather Vanes

417-C Ingalls Street, Santa Cruz, CA 95060

West Coast Weather Vanes creates handcrafted, limited edition copper and brass weather vanes for residential, commercial and public facilities and gardens. 250 designs available. Free product literature. Phone 800 762-8736. Fax 408 425-5505. E-Mail: wcwvanes@ix.netcom.com

Weathervanes

Windy Hill Forge

3824 Schroeder Ave., Perry Hall, MD 21128

Custom barn door strap hinges, large gate hinges, door hinges, bolts, hasps, cast iron wall washers. Restoration work on antique iron hardware. Phone 410 256-5890. E-Mail: windyhillforge@juno.com

New and Antique Forged Hardware

Woodcraft

P.O. Box 1686, Parkersburg, WV 26102

Woodcraft offers the highest quality woodworking tools including socket slicks, corner chisels, heavy duty framing chisels and adzes. Free catalog. Phone 800 225-1153. Fax 304 428-8271. Website: www.woodcraft.com

Woodworking Tools & Supplies

Wood's Metal Studios

6945 Fishburg Road, Huber Heights, OH 45424

Custom forging of traditional and contemporary ironwork, including gates, railings, stair rails, hardware, lighting, etc. Wood's Metal Studios can match antique hardware. Phone 937 233-6751

Reproduction Hardware, Gates & Railings

Woodstar Products, Inc.

1824 Hobbs Drive, P.O. Box 444, Delavan, WI 53115

One stop shopping for all of your horse stall needs. Woodstar offers doors, grills, hardware, swing-out feeders and stall mats. Free product literature. Phone 414 728-8460. Fax 414 728-1813. Website: www.wdstar.com

Stable Equipment, Barn Doors

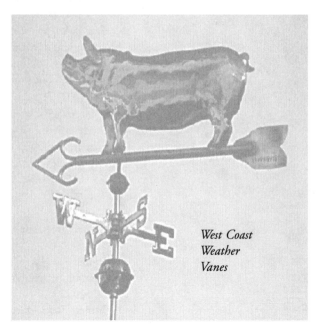

West Coast Weather Vanes

Barn Designs
5

An 1878 design from The Register of Rural Affairs, a New York farm journal

     The barns that you'll find on the next pages represent two great American building traditions: timber framing and building from mail-order plans. Three of the buildings are available as timber frames. Their post and beams are cut with mortise and tendon joints and delivered to your property. Then they are assembled and raised, by an old-fashioned bee, or with a modern crane, into your new barn. All of the rest of the barns are available as construction drawings that you can order from the designers.

     If you can't find a barn that suits you, check the selections of Stable Designs and Carriage Barn & Garage Designs in the chapters that follow this one. Most of the stables can be built as multi-purpose barns by simply omitting the interior partitions. All of the Carriage Barns are all-purpose buildings that you can use as barns.

Floor Space: 632 sq. ft.
Loft Space: 416 sq. ft.
Height of Ridge: 23'
Apparent Height: 18'-8"
Building Cost Range: $14,500 - $26,500
Light Frame Construction

Design #HD4

Cascade Barn

You can use the Cascade as a garage, a crafts barn, a studio or a workshop. Interior stairs lead to a bright and airy loft for an office or for high-and-dry storage. Plans, from **Homestead Design, Inc.**, include a list of materials for the structure and exterior shell. Order **Design #HD4** for $45.00.

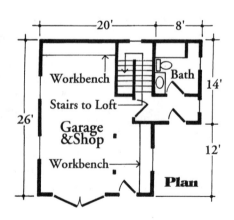

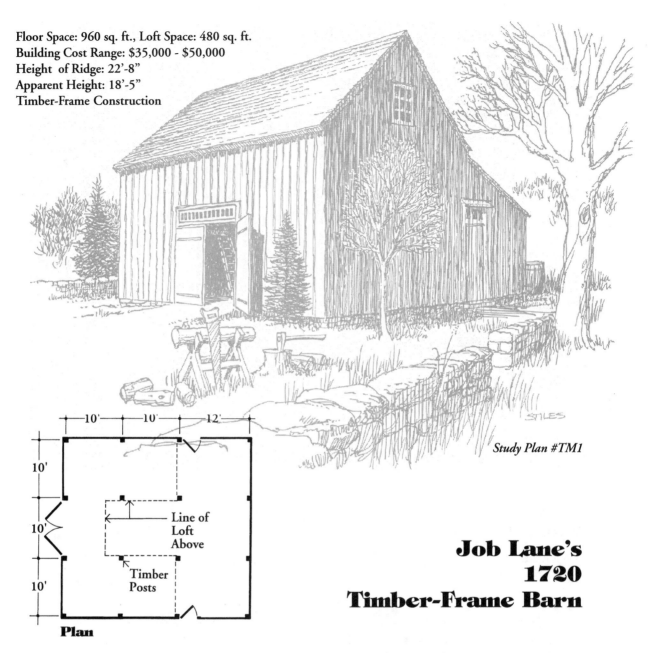

Floor Space: 960 sq. ft., Loft Space: 480 sq. ft.
Building Cost Range: $35,000 - $50,000
Height of Ridge: 22'-8"
Apparent Height: 18'-5"
Timber-Frame Construction

Study Plan #TM1

Line of Loft Above

Timber Posts

Plan

Job Lane's 1720 Timber-Frame Barn

Deacon Job Lane built his house in Bedford, Massachusetts in the early 1700s. His home, at 295 North Road, has been lovingly restored by the town and a group of dedicated volunteers called the Friends of the Job Lane House, Inc. It's now a landmark museum open to the public.

When the Friends decided to create a barn similar to the one that originally stood on the site, they asked timber framer Tom Musco to design it. Tom studied 17th century Eastern Massachusetts barns, their English precedents and the work of framer Job Lane, the deacon's grandfather. Tom cut a frame with authentic details: jowled posts, canted tie-beams, tapered rafters and naturally curved oak braces. The frame was raised in a traditional barn raising by the Bedford community.

The body of the barn is 30' wide, by 20' deep. It has a loft that's accessible by an open bay. A 12' deep, one-level shed stretches across the back.

Tom Musco's company, **Royalston Oak**, can create a custom frame on your property or provide an authentic old New England structure just like Job Lane's. Study plans of Job Lane's Barn and information about its history are available for $15.00. Order **Study Plan #TM1**.

Floor Space: 480 sq. ft.
Loft Space: 324 sq. ft.
Height of Ridge: 21'- 6"
Apparent Height: 17'-6"
Building Cost Range: $11,000 - $20,500
Light Frame Construction

Tillamook Barn

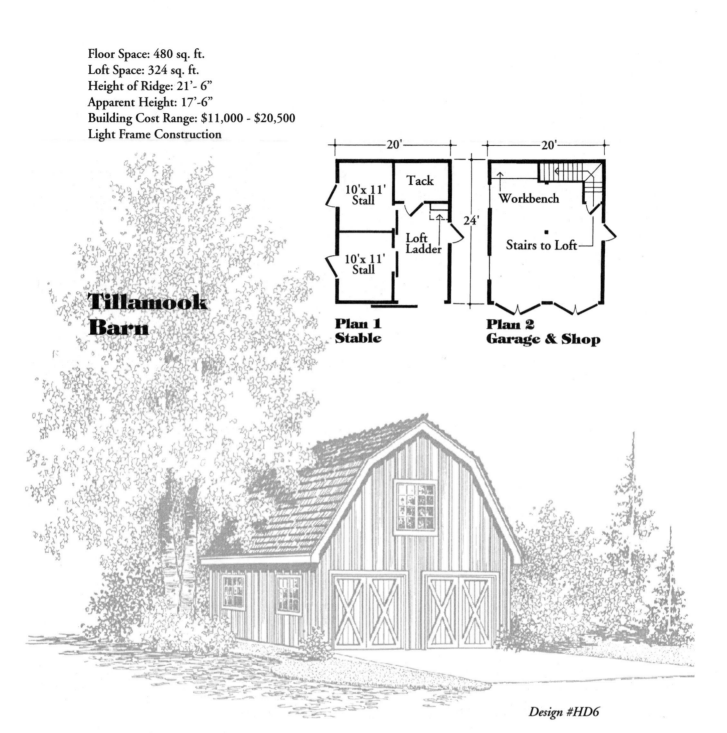

Plan 1 Stable

10'x 11' Stall	Tack
10'x 11' Stall	Loft Ladder

Plan 2 Garage & Shop

Workbench

Stairs to Loft

Design #HD6

The gambrel roof of the Tillamook barn creates a big storage loft. Build this barn as a stable with a hayloft or as a combination garage and shop with interior stairs up to an office or storage room.. Construction plans from **Homestead Design, Inc.** come with both plans shown and a list of materials for the structure and the exterior shell. Order **Design #HD6**, for $40.00.

Floor Space: 528 sq. ft.
Upper Level: 456 sq. ft.
Height of Ridge: 27'-10"
Apparent Height: 22'
Construction Cost Range: $24,500 - $33,000
Timber-Frame Construction

Study Plan #NW1

North Woods Timber-Frame Barn

The view above and the plans are just suggestions of what you can build on the North Woods frame. With a timber frame, exterior walls and interior partitions are built on a freestanding skeleton of wood posts and beams. You're free to create the interior layout and choose the exterior that you want.

This particular frame is tall and dramatic enough that it will look great under any exterior finishes. The 22' by 24' plan works well as a two bay garage, a small stable, a craft barn or any combination. The full-height upper level will make a fine hayloft, office or studio.

North Woods Joinery will create the frame, ship it to you and help you raise it. Your contractor can finish it into just the barn you need. Order **Study Plan #NW1** for $15.00 for complete information.

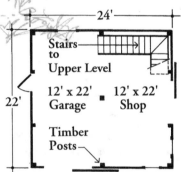

24'

Stairs to Upper Level

22'

12' x 22' Garage

12' x 22' Shop

Timber Posts

Plan 1 - Multi-Use Barn

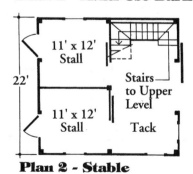

22'

11' x 12' Stall

11' x 12' Stall

Stairs to Upper Level

Tack

Plan 2 - Stable

Floor Space: 788 sq. ft.
Loft Space: 416 sq. ft.
Height of Ridge: 21'-6"
Apparent Height: 18'-2"
Building Cost Range: $17,000 - $30,500
Light Frame Construction

Winchester Barn

Design #HD12

This practical barn has a loft over half of its area and a high, open ceiling on the other half. The Winchester would make a great artist's studio or crafts barn, a generous two-car garage and shop or a fine stable with two stalls and a hayloft. Ten foot high sliding doors to the high bay make this ideal for parking an R.V., a tall truck or farm equipment. Order **Design #HD12**, for $45.00 from **Homestead Design, Inc.** The drawings come with a list of materials for the structure and exterior shell and both of the plans shown above.

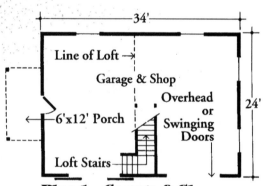

Plan 1 - Garage & Shop

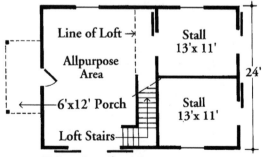

Plan 2 - Stable

Floor Space: 1,200 sq. ft.
Loft Space: 730 sq. ft.
Height of Ridge: 23'
Apparent Height: 17'
Height of Cupola: 32'
Building Cost Range: $44,000 - $70,000
Timber Frame Construction

Study Plan
#CO1

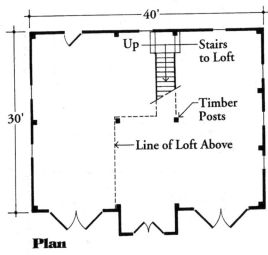

Plan

Chestnut Oak Timber Frame Barn

This pretty barn is just one of the countless variations that you can build on Chestnut Oak Company's 30'x40' timber frame. This design has three bays and a loft over half the space. It would be perfect as a studio or craft barn. The 30' building depth and wide side bays make this frame ideal to use as a shelter for trucks, campers or boats.

Chestnut Oak Co. will cut the timbers, ship them to you and help you raise them. You or your contractor can apply exterior finishes and interior partitions to suit your needs. **Study Plan #CO1** is available for $15.00.

Floor Space: 296 sq. ft.
Loft Crawl Space: 208 sq. ft.
Height of Ridge: 16'-9"
Apparent Height: 14'
Building Cost Range: $7,000 - $13,000
Light Frame Construction

Concord Barn

If you have a limited yard space or a limited budget, the little Concord barn might be just right for you. It won't limit your options. Build it as a garden shed, a workshop and small car garage, or as a stable. With each layout, you get a useful crawl-space storage loft. **Homestead Design, Inc.** includes plans for all three layouts with its complete building plans for just $40.00. Order **Design #HD3**.

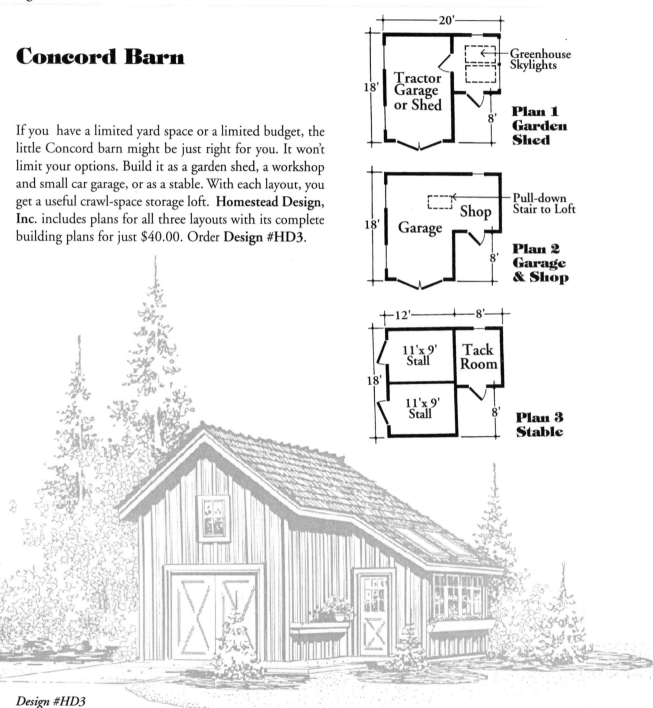

Design #HD3

Floor Space: 420 sq. ft.
Height of Ridge: 18'
Apparent Height: 14'-6"
Building Cost Range: $7,500 - $13,000
Light Frame Construction

Design #MR3

Little Barn

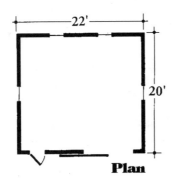

Plan

Designer **McKie Wing Roth** built this Little Barn as his own woodwork shop and as shelter for a big farm tractor. It's a great storage building or crafts barn and it could easily be fitted up as a two-stall stable. A wide sliding door opens on space that has 11'-10" clear headroom and no posts or obstructions. The structure is carried on the exterior walls so you're free to use all of the interior just as you need it. Windows are mounted 7'6" above the floor so you can use all of the wall space for storage. Construction plans for **Design #MR3** are available for $35.00.

Floor Space: 864 sq. ft.
Loft Storage: 684 sq. ft.
Height of Ridge 24'-6"
Height of Cupola 27'-2"
Apparent Height 20'
Building Cost Range: $22,500 - $39,000

Design #HD7

Cambridge Barn & Stable

The gambrel roof of this little barn creates a loft that has a full 8'-6" of headroom. The loft almost doubles the usable space in this building. It has convenient sliding access doors at both ends

Like many of **Homestead Design's** barns, a clever structural design with just two structural posts on the main floor gives you a variety of options with the floor plan. You can build the Cambridge with one, two or three stalls. Substitute a loft ladder for the walk-up stairs and you can squeeze in another pony. Or, leave areas open as a big workshop or equipment storage area.

Construction drawings for **Design #HD7** are priced at $60.00. They come with two different floor plans and a list of materials for the structure and exterior shell.

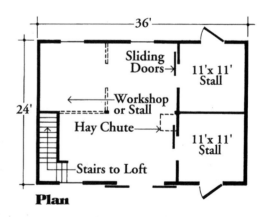

Plan

Stable Designs
6

You'll find a variety of stable designs on the following pages. Construction drawings for all of them can be ordered from their designers. Check the sections on Barn Designs and Carriage Barn and Garage Designs for more buildings that you can adapt for use as stables. You'll also find some attractive open sheds that make fine loafing sheds in the section on Shed and Garden Building Designs.

Most Victorian stables were built from mail-order plans.
This 1887 design is from a catalog titled Shoppell's Modern Houses

Floor Space: 1824 sq. ft., Loft Storage: 960 sq.ft.
Ridge Height: 22'-8", Apparent Height: 16'
Cupola Height: 34'
Building Cost Range: $28,000 - $45,000
Pole Frame Construction

Gambrell Roof Style
Design # SD10A

Monitor Roof Style
Design #SD10B

Gable Roof Style
Design #SD10C

Eight Stall Pole-Framed Stables

Any of the eight 12' x 12' stalls in this big barn can be fitted as a tack room, wash stall or feed room. A 20' wide loft runs the entire length of each of the building. It's open above all of the stalls for good ventilation and to allow you to easily drop hay. Big doors on both ends of the loft, located above the aisle doors allow easy loading of the loft from a truck bed.

This barn plan is available in three different styles. The Gambrel Roof Style, **Design #SD10A**, has the most loft storage. The Monitor Roof Style, **Design #SD10B**, allows additional light and ventilation with rows of loft windows. The Gable Roof Style, **Design #SD10C**, is the most economical to build.

Construction plans for each of the designs cost $99.00 from **Sheldon Designs, Inc.**

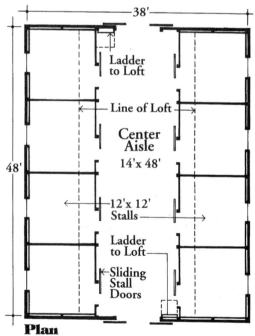

38'

Ladder to Loft

Line of Loft

Center Aisle
14'x 48'

48'

12'x 12' Stalls

Ladder to Loft

Sliding Stall Doors

Plan

Floor Space: 1512 sq. ft.
Loft Storage: 504 sq. ft.
Ridge Height: 19'
Apparent Height: 14'-6"
Cupola Height: 20'-6"
Building Cost Range: $27,500 - $50,000
Light Frame Construction

Design #HD11

Monterey
Six Stall Stable

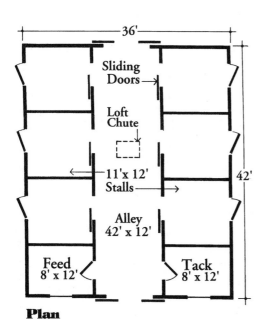

36'

Sliding
Doors →

Loft
Chute

← 11'x 12'
Stalls →

Alley
42' x 12'

42'

Feed
8' x 12'

Tack
8' x 12'

Plan

This big stable has a low pitch roof with shady overhangs. It's ideal for a warm weather location. Wide sliding barn doors at each end of the central Alley, outside doors for all stalls, big sliding windows, and an airy open loft all make for a comfortable, breezy interior. The loft runs above the Alley and has exterior access doors at each end. Besides the six stalls, there are two rooms that you can use for feed, tack, storage or as an office. The Monterey can be sided in inexpensive textured plywood with decorative vertical battens. Or, you can easily give it a more elegant look with clapboard siding.

Construction plans cost $90.00 and come with a list of materials for the exterior shell. Order **Design #HD11** from **Homestead Design, Inc.**

Covered Space: 400 sq. ft.
Height of Ridge: 15'
Apparent Height: 13'
Building Cost Range: $3,500 - $6,500
Timber Frame Construction

Loafing Shed

Design #RO3
Copyright, Russell Swinton Oatman

Use this simple 20'x20' building as a run-in shed or loafing shed. It might be all you need as a horse shelter if you live in a mild climate. The timber frame or post and beam structure allows you to easily alter the exterior and to add interior partitions. As shown, with sliding doors on one wall, the building can divide twoE fenced paddocks. However you use it, this little shed will be an attractive addition to your country place.

For construction drawings, order **Design #RO3**, for $25.00, from **Russell Swinton Oatman Design Associates, Inc.**

First Floor Space: 768 sq. ft.
Loft Storage: 320 sq. ft.
Height of Ridge: 17'-6"
Apparent Height: 14'-6"
Building Cost Range: $16,500 - $27,500
Light Frame Construction

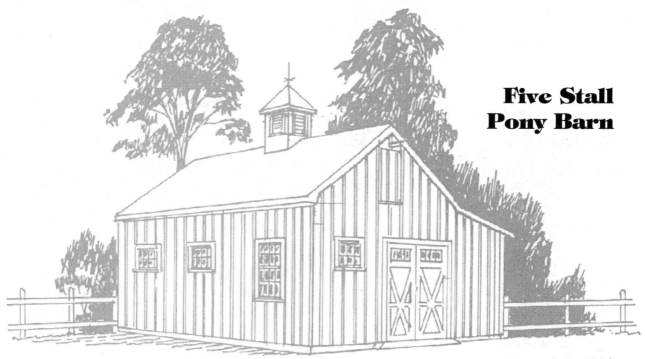

Five Stall Pony Barn

Design #RO4
Copyright, Russell Swinton Oatman

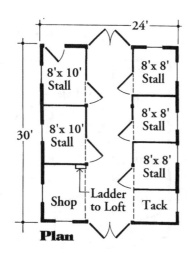

Plan

This efficient small barn is perfect for ponies and small animals. Architect Russell Oatman arranged stalls, a room for feed and tack, and a shop area along a convenient central aisle. Wide doors at both ends make easy maintenance and allow a summertime breeze. There is a loft above the center aisle that's accessible by an interior trapdoor and by an exterior hatch.

As you can see from the perspective drawing, the architect designed a simple shed roof over one of the rows of stalls. This reduces the overall height of the barn, saves cost in construction and gives a roof line that seems just right for a country setting.

Construction drawings cost $50.00. Order **Design #RO4** from **Russell Swinton Oatman Design Associates, Inc.**

Three Level Barn & Stable

First Floor Space: 1,200 sq. ft.
Second Floor Storage Space: 1,200 sq. ft.
Third Floor Loft: 400 sq. ft.
Height of Ridge: 31'-9"
Apparent Height: 22'-8"
Building Cost Range: $40,000 - $70,000
Light Frame Construction

Design #RO3
Copyright, Russell Swinton Oatman

This big barn follows the pattern adopted by New England farmers in the 19th century and popular there ever since. The first floor is divided into stalls, a tack room, a room for grain and feed and a large center aisle. Doors at both ends of the aisle allow easy maintenance and good ventilation. There are stairs up to a full second floor for hay or storage and another set of stairs to a third level loft.

The view above shows the barn set into a hillside with an additional lower level. That's just one of the many custom features that **Russell Swinton Oatman Design Associates, Inc.** can create from their standard design. Complete construction plans for the standard Three Level Barn & Stable are $100.00. Order **Design #RO4.**

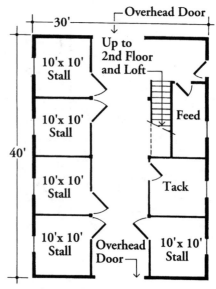

First Floor Plan

Floor Space, Plan 1: 288 sq. ft.
Floor Space, Plan 2: 360 sq. sf.
Height of Ridge: 15'-6"
Height of Cupola: 17'-4"
Apparent Height: 11'-4"
Building Cost Range: $3,500 - $7,000
Pole Frame Construction

Design #HD8

Prescott
One or Two Stall
Pole Frame Stable

Start with one stall, then add another when you need it. With the Prescott, a grid of poles supports the wide roof and allows you to build a variety of layouts. Construction drawings from **Homestead Design Inc.**, come with both plans shown and a list of materials for the building shell. Plans for **Design #HD8** cost $40.00.

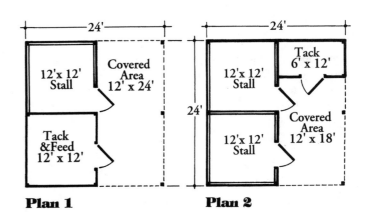

Plan 1

Plan 2

Floor Space: 936 sq. ft., Loft Storage: 748 sq. ft.
Building Cost Range: $17,000 - $27,000
Ridge Height: 19'-10"
Cupola Height: 28'-6"
Apparent Height: 14'-6"
Pole Frame Const.

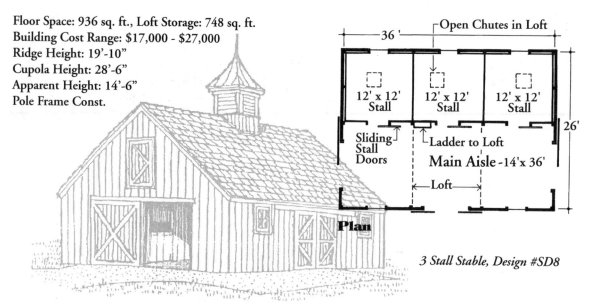

3 Stall Stable, Design #SD8

Pole Frame Stables

Either of these two efficient pole framed stables will look great on your property. Architect Andy Sheldon has given them great proportions, simple barn-style details, easy-to-build pole framing and common sense working layouts. As pole buildings, these can be easily adapted to suit your specific needs with changes to the interior layouts and your choice of exterior finishes. Construction plans for either design are $79.00 from **Sheldon Designs, Inc.**

Design #SD8, shown above, features three 12' x 12' stalls and a big aisle for a workroom, grooming area and storage. The aisle opens to your yards, paddocks or driveways with three sliding doors. A U-shaped loft is open at the center of the aisle for easy loading. Chutes above each of the stalls are for hay and ventilation. You could use one of the stalls as a generous sized tack and feed room.

Design #SD9, below, has two stalls but could easily be fitted with four. Sliding doors at each end allow a breeze through the center aisle and easy clean-outs. The areas above the stalls and the multi-purpose room are storage lofts, each with an outside access hatch. Although this is shown as a stable, this traditional barn plan has an infinite variety of uses.

Floor Space: 912 sq. ft., Loft Storage: 576 sq. ft.
Building Cost Range: $15,000 - $24,000
Ridge Height: 22'-6"
Cupola Height: 31-0"
Apparent Height: 15'-8"
Pole Frame Const.

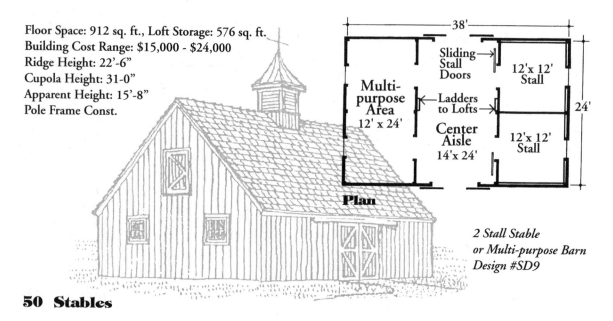

*2 Stall Stable
or Multi-purpose Barn
Design #SD9*

Floor Space: 1,296 sq. ft.
Loft Storage: 576 sq. ft.
Ridge Height: 23'-6"
Apparent Height: 20'-10"
Building Cost Range: $27,000 - $47,000
Light Frame Construction

Design #HD10

Austin Five Stall Stable

Homestead Design's Austin barn features a monitor roof, a high and bright loft, five box stalls and a room for feed, tack and storage. The loft runs over the central Alley and extends over each of the stalls. It's open to the stalls below to allow ventilation and an easy job of dropping hay and bedding. There is a big sliding door at each end of the Alley and a loft doors above each of those. Headroom is a full 9' on both the main floor level and in the loft. Complete construction plans for **Design #HD10** are available for $90.00.

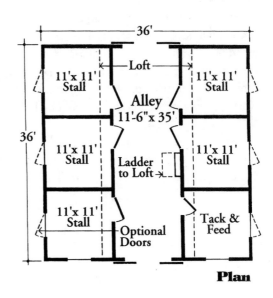

Plan

Floor Space: 864 sq. ft.
Loft Storage: 432 sq. ft.
Ridge Height: 21'-3"
Apparent Height: 19'-4"
Building Cost Range: $18,500 - $32,500
Light Frame Construction

Lancaster
Two or Three Stall
Stable

Design #HD9

You can build the Lancaster barn just the way you need it. The two layouts shown are provided with the construction plans, but you can design your own interior plan without upsetting the engineering. The exterior walls and four freestanding interior posts take the weight of the loft and the roof. That lets you arrange and rearrange the interior partitions without worry. Grab a pencil and start sketching !

Construction plans and a list of materials for the structure and exterior shell are available for $60.00 from **Homestead Design Inc.** Order **Design #HD9.**

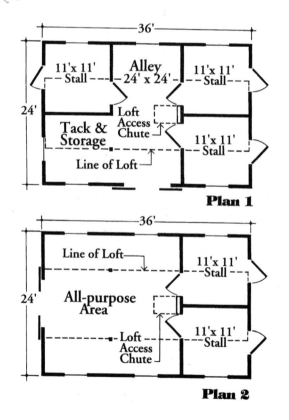

Carriage Barn & Garage Designs
7

*A carriage house design from the 1895 plan catalog
How to Build, Furnish & Decorate*

The buildings on the following pages can serve as shelters for your cars, trucks, tractors or boats. They offer something more than most conventional garages both in style and in features. Many have attached sheds and shops and a few are designed to expand easily as your needs change.

Each design has a convenient loft. An upper level on a garage doubles the useful storage space at a minimum cost. Lofts use space that's usually wasted. They don't need any additional roof surface or foundations, so you're just building a floor and stairs. And, the space that you gain is high and dry. It's perfect for paper records, clothing and books - all items that you might worry about in a one level garage. Throw the lawn toys and pool tubes up there in winter and the sleds and snow shovels in summer and you'll have much more room in the garage below.

Many of the Barn Designs and a few of the Stable Designs on the previous pages will also make great carriage barns. Some are designed with garage parking bays or with alternate plans so that you can use them for parking. Page back through those sections for more possibilities.

Floor Space: 762 sq. ft., Loft Storage: 418 sq. ft.
Ridge Height: 23'-4"
Cupola Height: 27'-8"
Apparent Height: 18'-6"
Building Cost Range: $19,000 - $35,000
Light Frame and Masonry Construction

Design #AW1

1887
Carriage House

Architect **Anthony Wolfe** got his inspiration for this little barn from an 1887 carriage house. Then he carefully modified the sizes of the spaces, doors and windows to create a building that works today. There's a generous sized garage, a large, separate area for a shop or garden tool storage and a walk-up storage loft with an exterior hatch. Build this to complement a Victorian or Shingle Style home. Plans for **Design #AW1** are available for $60.00.

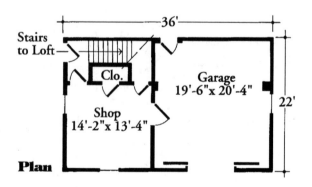

Stairs to Loft

Clo.

Garage
19'-6"x 20'-4"

Shop
14'-2"x 13'-4"

36'

22'

Plan

Floor Space: 608 sq. ft., Loft Storage: 424 sq. ft.
Building Cost Range: $11,500 - $17,500
Ridge Height: 19'-4"
Cupola Height: 27'-8"
Apparent Height: 18'-6"
Pole Frame Construction

All-Purpose Pole Barn

Design #SD7

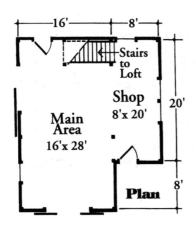

You'll find plenty of storage space and a nice, flexible layout in this little pole framed barn. Use this as a garage and workshop, a crafts barn or as a shelter for tractors or small boats. There is a full set of stairs to a loft. The gambrel roof allows plenty of storage space and 6'-8" loft headroom. Headroom in the main area below is generous at 9'0". Two walk doors and two big sliding doors add to the flexibility of this layout. Because this is a pole barn, it's easy to build and easy to modify to your specific needs.

You can order detailed building plans of **Design #SD7** for $69.00 from **Sheldon Designs, Inc.**

Floor Area: 880 sq. ft.
Building Cost Range: $19,000 - $27,000
Ridge Height: 21'-6"
Apparent Height: 14'-8"
Light Frame Construction

Hip roof Style
Design #SD6C

Gable Roof Style
Design #SD6A

Saltbox Style
Design #SD6B

Gambrel Roof Style
Design #SD6D

Great Three Car Garages

These are great garages because of their good proportions, concise construction plans and convenient storage lofts. You can pick the style that goes with your home and then select siding and a roof that matches. Building plans for any of the three car garages shown above cost $59.00 from **Sheldon Designs, Inc.** Use the Design numbers shown above to specify your selection of roof style.

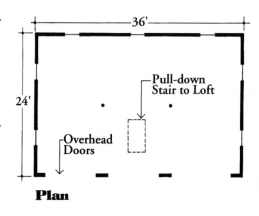

36'

24'

Pull-down
Stair to Loft

Overhead
Doors

Plan

Floor Area: 540 sq. ft.
Building Cost Range: $12,000 - $20,000
Ridge Height: 21'-6"
Apparent Height: 14'-8"
Light Frame Construction

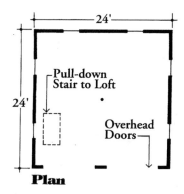

Plan

24'

24'

Pull-down
Stair to Loft

Overhead
Doors

Like the three car garages on the opposite page, these two car designs feature good looks, accurate construction plans and convenient lofts with pull-down stairs. You can pick from four roof styles. Building plans for any of the styles cost $49.00 from **Sheldon Designs, Inc.** When ordering, please specify your choice of roof style by using the Design number in the illustration below.

Great Two Car Garages

*Saltbox Style
Design #SD5B*

*Gambrel Roof Style
Design #SD5D*

*Hip Roof Style
Design #SD5C*

*Gable Roof Style
Design #SD5A*

Floor Space: 936 sq. ft.
Loft Storage: 525 sq. ft.
Height of Ridge: 23'
Apparent Height: 19'-10"
Building Cost Range: $21,500 - $36,000
Light Frame Construction

Kensington
Three Bay Garage

Design #HD2

The Kensington is a saltbox style garage with space for three big cars, a workbench and plenty of storage. An exterior staircase leads to a loft with 9' headroom. This design reverses the usual saltbox layout - the front here is the lowest side of the building. This tends to visually reduce the size of a building when seen from the front. The Kensington is a big garage that won't seem out of scale in a residential neighborhood.

Plans cost $60.00 and include a list of materials. Order **Design #HD2** from **Homestead Design, Inc.**

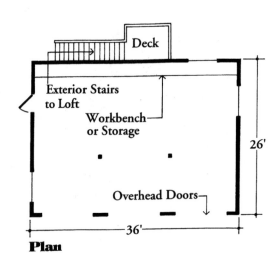

Plan

Floor Space: 412 sq. ft.
Loft Space: 302 sq. ft.
Height of Ridge: 19'-6"
Apparent Height: 16'
Building Cost Range: $8,500 - $11,500
Pole Frame Construction

Ashokan Carriage Barn

Design #DB1

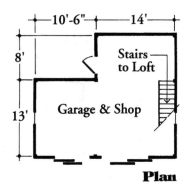

Plan

This little pole-framed barn will store a surprising amount. One large parking bay will fit your car, truck or boat. Another smaller one will fit a lawn tractor and a workbench. There's an easy walk-up to a full loft for seasonal tools, holiday decorations and anything else that you can't fit in your attic. Bikes and garden tools fit under the stairs. Two sets of sliding doors stack out of the way. An outside hatch and a lifting post help in getting bulky items up into the loft.

Order construction drawings for **Design #DB1** for $36.00, from **Donald J. Berg, AIA.**

Floor Space: 384 sq. ft.
Floor Space with Shed Addition: 624 sq. ft.
Loft Space: 300 sq. ft.
Height of Ridge: 21'-6"
Apparent Height: 17'-4"
Building Cost Range: $9,500 - $23,500
Light Frame Construction

Design #HD5

Pilchuck Barn

The classic lines of this simple barn will make it look great on your country property. Build a 16' x 24' barn, garage or shop and then expand with a pretty shed addition for horse stalls or storage. Construction drawings come with all three plans shown. Order **Design #HD5** for $45.00 from **Homestead Design, Inc.**

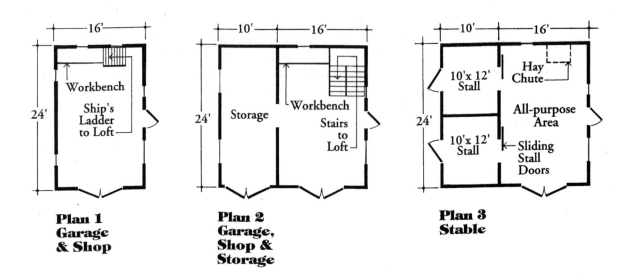

**Plan 1
Garage
& Shop**

**Plan 2
Garage,
Shop &
Storage**

**Plan 3
Stable**

Floor Space: 440 sq. ft.
Loft Storage: 210 sq. ft.
Height of Ridge: 18'-6"
Apparent Height: 14'
Building Cost Range: $10,000 - $16,500
Light Frame Construction

Design #MR2

Stonetree Buggy Barn

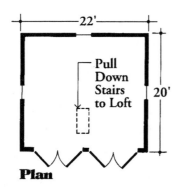

Designer **McKie Wing Roth's** Stonetree barn has the layout of a conventional garage, but there is nothing ordinary in the details. A high-pitched roof gives graceful proportions and space for a convenient storage loft. The loft is accessed by pull-down stairs. Hinged barn doors below a copper-lined vee-gutter give a traditional, timeless look. Plans for Design #MR2 are priced at $35.00.

Designs #MR1 and #MR2 Combined

4 Bay Carriage Barns

Stretching a garage out to fit four cars often makes an ungainly building. You protect your vehicles but damage the look of your property. Here's a way to have four parking bays in a pretty backbuilding. Build designer **McKie Wing Roth's** Stockbridge Barn, from the next page, with his Stonetree Buggy Barn, from the previous one. The two structures have the same roof pitch and similar details. Built side-by-side they take on the appearance of a rambling old barn. You'll have plenty of space for parking, storage or a workshop, a big loft, and a building that looks great in the countryside.

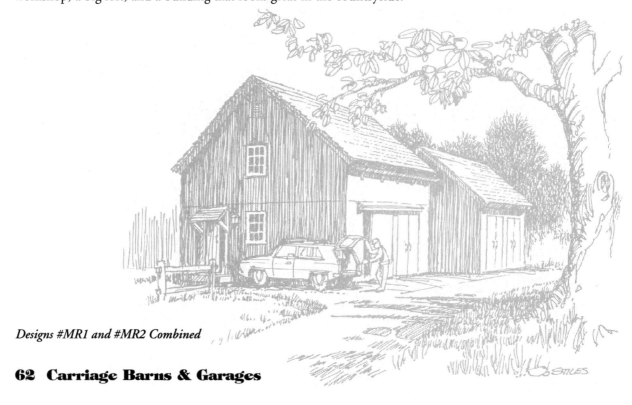

Designs #MR1 and #MR2 Combined

Floor Space: 624 sq. ft.
Loft Storage: 588 sq. ft.
Height of Ridge: 25'
Apparent Height: 19'-6"
Building Cost Range: $18,500 - $30,500
Light Frame Construction

Stockbridge Buggy Barn

Design #MR1

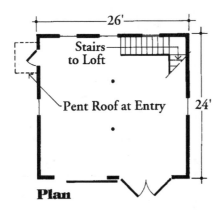

Plan

26'
24'

Stairs to Loft

Pent Roof at Entry

The Stockbridge is an allpurpose backbuilding. You can build it as a garage, a small barn, or a workshop. There's a walk-up loft with 8' headroom and skylights at the back. You can use it as an office or studio. A combination of doors open to the lower level. A pair of hinged barn doors front one bay while a large sliding door serves the other. The sliding door glides in front of the hinged ones and is protected from rain by a track cover and wooden vee-gutter. A walk-in door is protected by a pretty shed roof. The details and proportions are traditional and timeless.

Complete construction drawings are available for $50.00. Order **Design #MR1** from **McKie Wing Roth, Jr. Designer, Inc.**

Floor Space: 660 sq. ft.
Loft Space: 480 sq. ft.
Height of Ridge: 21'
Apparent Height: 17'
Building Cost Range: $16,000 - $29,500
Light Frame Construction

Westport
All-Purpose Garage

Design #HD1

Here's a design that can't be beat for versatility. It's a two-car garage and shop that can be easily expanded to fit three cars and a bigger shop area. There's an interior staircase to a big loft with plenty of storage room. With the optional bathroom and bright skylights the loft would make a fine studio or office. The combination of an office with the generous first floor area makes this ideal for a craft or repair shop business.

Drawings for **Design #HD1** cost $60.00, from **Homestead Design, Inc.** They include two floor plans and a list of materials for the basic shell.

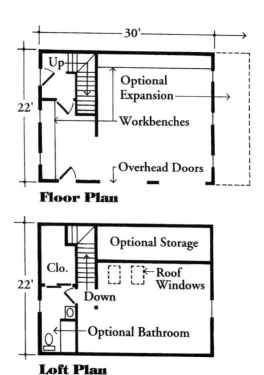

Floor Space: 480 sq. ft.
Loft Space: 330 sq. ft.
Height of Ridge: 20'
Apparent Height: 14'-6"
Building Cost Range: $9,500 - $13,000
Pole Frame Construction

Design #DB3

Battenkill Pole Barn

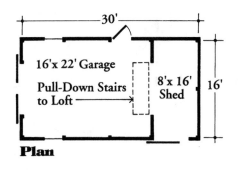

Plan

30'

16' x 22' Garage

Pull-Down Stairs to Loft →

8' x 16' Shed

16'

Add a loft and a little shed to a one bay garage and you have a remarkably useful little barn. Use the parking bay for your car, truck or canoes, and park your tractor, bikes, snowmobiles or ATVs in the shed. Or, you can add skylights to the shed roof to create a bright workshop or potting shed. Order construction plans for **Design #DB3**, for $36.00, from **Donald J. Berg, AIA.**

Floor Space: 576 sq. ft.
Loft Space: 288 sq. ft.
Covered Wood Shed: 120 sq. ft.
Height of Ridge: 22'
Apparent Height: 15'-6"
Building Cost Range: $13,000 - $23,500
Light Frame Construction

Design #RO1
Copyright, Russell Swinton Oatman

New England Style Garage & Woodshed

This elegant garage by architect Russell Swinton Oatman was designed to complement a New England Colonial or Cape Cod style home. It has generous space for two cars, a walk-up storage loft and a covered wood shed that runs the full length of one side.

Construction drawings are available for $50.00. Order **Design #RO1** directly from **Russell Swinton Oatman Design Associates, Inc.**

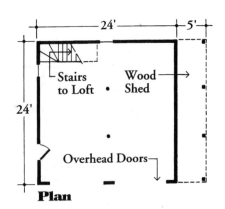

Floor Space: 576 sq. ft.
Loft Space: 288 sq. ft.
Height of Ridge: 22'
Apparent Height: 15'-6"
Building Cost Range: $12,500 - $22,000
Light Frame Construction

Design #RO2
Copyright, Russell Swinton Oatman

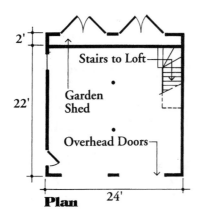

Plan

New England Style Garage & Garden Shed

Like the garage on the facing page, this pretty design will look great with a Colonial or Cape Cod home. It features two full-size parking bays and stairs to a high storage loft. Across the back, there's a useful shed for yard tools and toys. Fit that shed with glass doors and shelves and build it to face the sun and you'll have a prefect potting shed.

Construction drawings for **Design #RO2** are available from **Russell Swinton Oatman Design Associates, Inc.** for $50.00.

Floor Space: 352 sq. ft.
Loft Space: 330 sq. ft.
Height of Ridge: 20'-4'''
Apparent Height: 14'-8"
Building Cost Range: $7,500 - $11,500
Pole Frame Construction

Design #DB2

One Bay Country Garage

This simple one bay garage is designed for inexpensive pole frame construction. Add a cupola from one of the manufacturers that you'll find in this book's Directory and you'll have an attractive country building at a very reasonable price. Plans of **Design #DB2** cost $36.00 from **Donald J. Berg, AIA.**

Plan

Floor Space: 1,200 sq. ft.
Loft Space: 1,160 sq. ft.
Height of Ridge: 26'
Height of Cupola: 31'-4"
Apparent Height: 19'-6"
Building Cost Range: $32,500 - $55,000
Light Frame Construction

Design #JO3

Country Classic Three Bay Garage

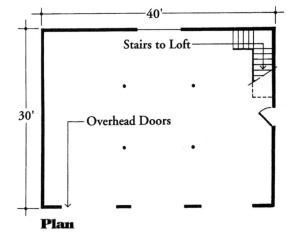

This three bay garage will swallow up everything that you need to store. This is one of the biggest garages that you'll find. The first level can park a car, a camper and a boat on its trailer. The big walk-up loft can serve as additional storage, as an office or as a studio. Like a pretty barn, the good proportions of this building let it look great with even the simplest of finishes.

Complete construction drawings cost $65.00 from **Just Outbuildings**. Order **Design #JO3**.

Floor Space: 432 sq. ft.
Loft Space: 400 sq. ft.
Height of Ridge: 22'-8"
Apparent Height: 18'-6"
Building Cost Range: $11,000 - $19,500
Light Frame Construction

Design #JO2

One Bay Garage & Barn

Board & batten siding, simple details, a loft hatch and barn sash windows at the back give this little building the look of a country barn. An open plan and convenient walk-up loft give it the versatility of a barn. Use it as a one car garage and you'll have space to spare for a lawn tractor, garden tools and bikes.

Just Outbuildings offers construction drawings of Design #JO2, for $40.00.

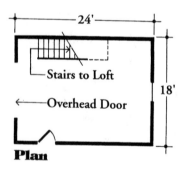

Floor Space: 512 sq. ft.
Loft Space: 350 sq. ft.
Height of Ridge: 21'-6"
Apparent Height: 16'-6"
Building Cost Range: $10,000 - $13,500
Pole Frame Construction

Design #DB4

Cold Spring Pole Barn

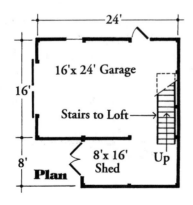

One parking bay and a small shed extension might be all the storage you need. This efficient little pole barn will hold a car, bikes and yard tools. The shed will park a big yard tractor or house a workshop, and there are stairs to a loft for even more storage. Plans for **Design #DB4** cost $36.00 from **Donald J. Berg, AIA.**

Floor Space: 576 sq. ft.
Loft Space: 370 sq. ft.
Height of Ridge: 24'-6"
Height of Cupola: 28'-6"
Apparent Height: 21'
Building Cost Range: $16,500 - $30,000
Light Frame Construction

Design #JO5

Gambrel Garage

This elegant two bay garage would grace a country estate or suburban street. The steeply pitched gambrel roof ends in gently curved "flying eaves" at the bottom. Clapboard siding and classic details add to the charm. The steep roof allows a high loft that would make a great office or studio. Windows at both ends and dormer windows on both sides brighten the space.

Just Outbuildings offers carefully detailed construction drawings of **Design #JO5** for $65.00.

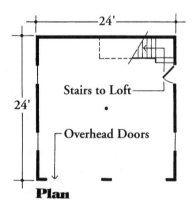

Stairs to Loft

Overhead Doors

Plan

Sheds & Garden Building Designs
8

This dog house design appeared in America's first book of mail-order plans,
Village and Farm Cottages, which was published in 1856 by architects
Henry Cleaveland, William Backus and Samuel Backus.

      Sheds and garden buildings are available in all styles from a great variety of sources. Check the Directory of Products and Services, starting on page 17, for sources of prefabricated gazebos, arbors, sheds, mailboxes and birdhouses. Factory-built garden structures like the ones that you'll find listed offer great quality at a reasonable price. Some of the manufactures offer easy-to-build kits while others will deliver complete sheds right to your yard.

      The designs that you'll find on the next few pages are here because they are different than anything that you'll find through the Directory or at your lumberyard. The Garden Pavilion is bigger than you'll usually find and the pool house is more elaborate than anything you can order from a factory. The playhouses are do-it-yourself projects. Most of the sheds are designed for inexpensive pole building construction. You should be able to have them built on your property at a much lower price than any other permanent building of the same size. The sheds are available in a variety roof styles, so you can pick the one that matches your home.

Enclosed Floor Space: 200 sq. ft.
Courtyard: 648 sq. ft.
Height of Ridge: 12'-8"
Height of Cupola: 15'
Apparent Height: 10'-6"
Building Cost Range: $9,500 - $17,000
Light Frame Construction

Design #JO4

Classic Cabana

Turn your backyard into a comfortable and elegant living area with this pool-side or beach-front cabana. The paved courtyard is partly covered by a roof and partly by a shady trellis. The sunny eating area has two sets of French doors. It has room for kitchen cabinets and appliances, and a table. There's a bath and dressing room and enough additional space for pool equipment or storage.

Construction drawings are priced at $35.00. Order **Design #JO4** from **Just Outbuildings**.

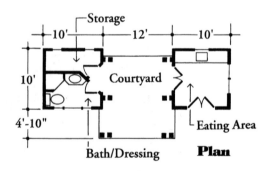

Covered Area: 380 sq. ft.
Overall Height: 26'-4"
Apparent Height: 17'-6"
Building Cost Range: $7,500 - $13,500
Light Frame Roof Construction

Design #JO1

Garden Pavilion

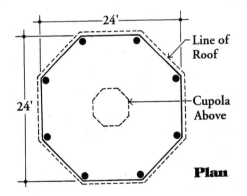

24'

24'

Line of Roof

Cupola Above

Plan

A dramatic octagonal roof is supported by eight classic columns in this creation from **Just Outbuildings**. This pavilion is big enough to be a community band shell. Or, you can use it as an outdoor living room on your property. Building plans for **Design #JO1** cost $45.00.

20' Design - Floor Space: 320 sq. ft.
Cost Range: $3,500 - $5,000
Pole Frame Construction
Ridge Height :16'-6"
Apparent Height: 12'

16' Design - Floor Space: 256 sq. ft.
Cost Range: $3,000 - $4,500
Pole Frame Construction
Ridge Height: 16'-6"
Apparent Height: 12'

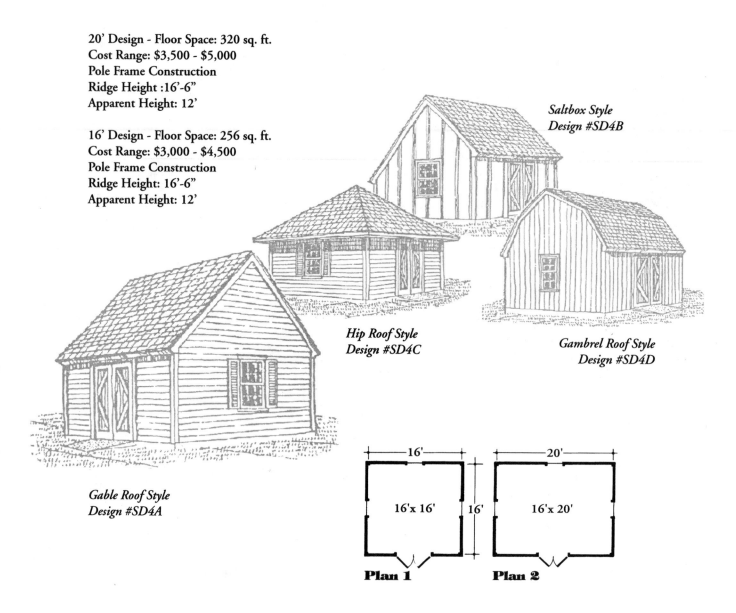

Saltbox Style
Design #SD4B

Hip Roof Style
Design #SD4C

Gambrel Roof Style
Design #SD4D

Gable Roof Style
Design #SD4A

Plan 1 — 16' — 16'x 16' — 16'

Plan 2 — 20' — 16'x 20'

16' Wide Pole Frame Sheds

Any of these 16' wide pole-framed buildings can serve as a large storage shed, a workshop, a small barn, a garage for your tractor, a craft shop or as a roadside farm stand. You can choose the roof style that complements your home and use siding and roof shingles that match.

Construction drawings are available from **Sheldon Designs, Inc.** for each of the roof styles shown. The drawings for each style come with both of the floor plans shown above and are priced at $44.00. When ordering, please make sure to specify the roof style you need.

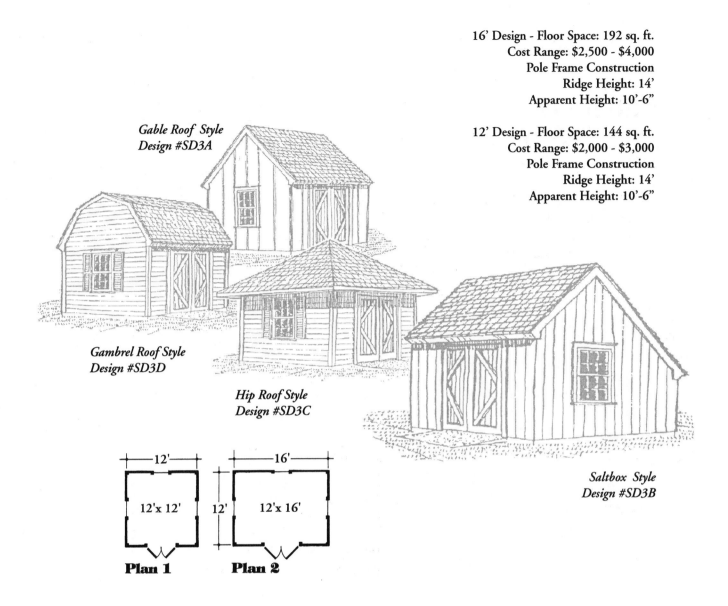

16' Design - Floor Space: 192 sq. ft.
Cost Range: $2,500 - $4,000
Pole Frame Construction
Ridge Height: 14'
Apparent Height: 10'-6"

12' Design - Floor Space: 144 sq. ft.
Cost Range: $2,000 - $3,000
Pole Frame Construction
Ridge Height: 14'
Apparent Height: 10'-6"

Gable Roof Style
Design #SD3A

Gambrel Roof Style
Design #SD3D

Hip Roof Style
Design #SD3C

Saltbox Style
Design #SD3B

12'
12'x 12'
Plan 1

16'
12'
12'x 16'
Plan 2

12' Wide Pole Frame Sheds

These 12' wide pole-framed buildings are a good size for your use as a storage shed, a small workshop, a shelter for a lawn tractor and bikes, and a place for all your yard tools. Just choose the style you like.

Concise building plans are available for each of the roof styles shown for $39.00 from **Sheldon Designs, Inc.** The drawings for each style come with both the 12' x 12' floor plan and the 12' x 16' layout. Specify the Design number listed in the illustration above for the roof style you want.

Do it yourself projects
Cost of Materials: $150 - $500

Children's Playhouses

Build one of these playhouses and make some child very happy. Imagination will turn the Three-Legged Playhouse, at right, into a lookout tower or a pirate ship. The Traditional Playhouse, below, will be someone's play school house, clubhouse and hideaway. Both buildings are great for backyard camp-outs.

The Three-Legged playhouse is a great do-it-yourself project. The Traditional Playhouse is for a parent or grandparent with a bit of experience with power tools. You can build it in pieces in your basement or garage and then assemble it in the yard.

Plan

Design #ST4

Design #ST3

For construction drawings of the Traditional Playhouse, order **Design #ST3** for $25.00. For your prints of the Three-Legged Playhouse, order **Design #ST4** for $20.00. Both are by **Stiles Designs** and both are easy to follow for weekend builders. .

Plan
—Covered Porch

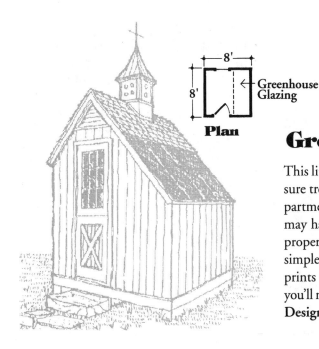

Plan

Greenhouse Glazing

Floor Space: 64 sq. ft.
Height of Ridge: 10' Cupola Height: 14'
Cost Range: $1,200 - $2,000
Light Frame Construction

Greenhouse & Garden Shed

This little greenhouse and garden shed is built on skids of pressure treated wood. Many community zoning and building departments will consider this a temporary structure so that you may have more flexibility on where you can locate it on your property. 2x4 framing, clear and accurate building plans, and simple details make this a great do it yourself project. Blueprints cost just $19.00 and come with a list of the materials you'll need for construction. Order **Design #SD1** from **Sheldon Designs, Inc.**

8' Design - Floor Space: 64 sq. ft.
12' Design - Floor Space: 96 sq. ft.
16' Design - Floor Space: 128 sq. ft.
Cost Range: $1,000 - $3,000
Pole Frame Construction
Ridge Height: 12'-6"
Apparent Height: 9'-8"

Pole Frame Sheds

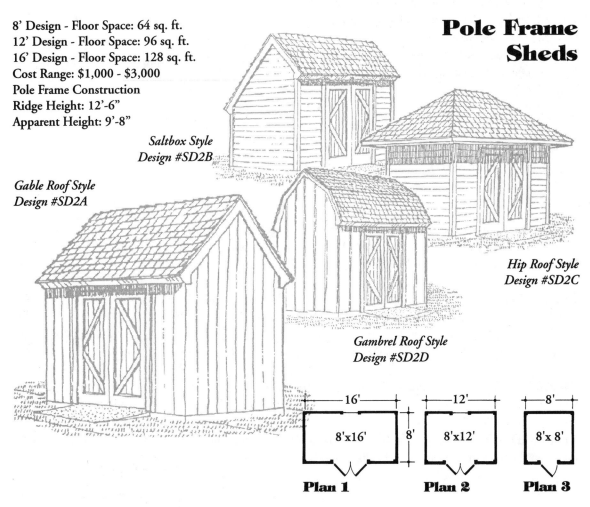

Saltbox Style
Design #SD2B

Gable Roof Style
Design #SD2A

Hip Roof Style
Design #SD2C

Gambrel Roof Style
Design #SD2D

Plan 1 — 16' — 8' — 8'x16'

Plan 2 — 12' — 8'x12'

Plan 3 — 8' — 8'x 8'

Construction plans are available from **Sheldon Designs, Inc.** for each of the four styles shown. Building drawings for each style present all three of the plan sizes shown above and are priced at $34.00. Please specify the roof style that you want by using the Design number shown in the illustration above.

Pole Frame Utility Sheds

Three Bay Design - Covered Area: 600 sq. ft.
Two Bay Design - Covered Area: 400 sq. ft.
Cost Range: $4,500 - $10,500
Height of Ridge: 23'
Apparent Height: 15'
Pole Frame Construction

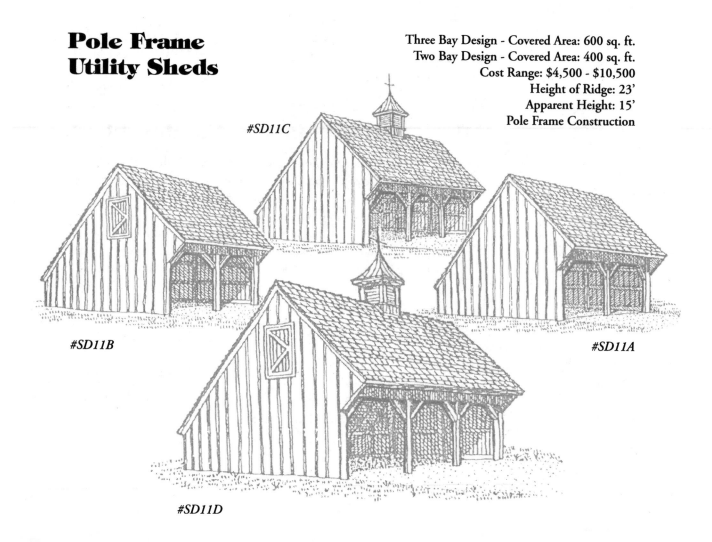

#SD11C

#SD11B

#SD11A

#SD11D

These easy-to-build pole structures make great shelters for farm equipment and lumber. They are ideal loafing sheds for horses. Open, as shown, any of the designs will be a fine carport; add doors and you'll have a pretty garage. Order building plans from **Sheldon Designs, Inc.**

Design #SD11A is a two bay, 20' x 20' shelter with 10' inside height. Construction plans are $39.00.

Design #SD11B is also a 20' x 20', two bay design but it has a full-length storage loft with 6'-8" headroom and an access door. Inside height on the lower level is 8'. Construction drawings are $39.00.

Design #SD11C has three open bays and a sheltered area of 20' x 30'. Inside height is 10'. Plans cost $44.00.

Design #SD11D is 20' x 30' with three bays and a full-length loft with an access door. Headroom is 8' in the open shelter and 6'-8" in the loft. Plans are $44.00.

Plans for all of the designs in the last four chapters are available directly from their designers. There are three types of plans that you can order: construction drawings that are prepared for use by an experienced builder, do-it-yourself plans, and study plans of timber-frame kits.

Study Plans of Timber Frame Designs

You'll find some designs in this book that are available as pre-cut kits of framing timbers. These are traditional wood post and beam structures with sophisticated mortise and tendon joints. The artisans who design them will cut them for you and ship them to your site. They'll coordinate with your foundation contractor, supervise the assembly and "barn-raising", and leave you with the biggest and most beautiful piece of site sculpture your neighborhood has seen in a hundred years. With the frame in place, you or your carpenters can apply the roofing, siding, doors and windows to turn it into a showplace barn or stable.

The Study Plans that you can purchase are usually scale drawings showing the general layout of the timbers and suggestions for exterior elevations and interior partitions. You can use the drawings to plan the building on your site and to get estimates on the foundation and finish construction. Your study plans will include information on how you can order your frame.

Do It Yourself Plans

A few of the designs in this book were created as do-it-yourself projects. Their drawings tend to have additional details, lists of materials, or step-by-step instructions for building. They're made for the weekend builder with some experience with woodworking and with access to power tools. Do-it-yourself plans are also perfectly suitable for use by professional builders: in fact, they will make the work and the chore of estimating costs a lot easier. You'll see a note in the description of a design if the drawings are suitable for do-it-yourself projects.

Construction Plans

Most of the designs presented in this book are available as construction drawings, prepared for use by experienced builders. Mail-order plans can reduce your cost of securing a great building design. For a custom design by a building professional, even of a simple barn, stable or shed, you can expect to spend a few hundred to several thousand dollars, depending on your project's size and complexity. A designer has to spend many hours conceiving and engineering a building and then drawing the plans.

With pre-designed buildings, and pre-drawn plans, you're getting the advantage of a professional's expertise at a fraction of the cost. But, there are considerations that you have to weigh.

Mail-order designs usually meet national codes and standards at the time they are drawn. Codes change constantly and local ordinances are sometimes different than national standards. In addition, mail-order designs are usually aimed at average soil and climatic conditions. Your building may need to be adapted to meet current codes in your community and to suit your soil and climate.

The changes are often very simple and can be handled by your builder in the normal course of construction. But, to be safe, you should always have mail-order plans reviewed by a local architect, construction engineer or licensed building designer prior to construction. Your contractor and local building department officials will usually have names that they can recommend.

Some small sheds and agricultural buildings don't need permits, but most backbuildings do. Check with your community's building and zoning officials, and secure all necessary permits before starting construction.

What the Construction Drawings Include

All of the drawings for designs in this book include scaled plans, sections and exterior elevations. They also include the details, notes and dimensions needed to build. Since the drawings are prepared for use by experienced builders, they use standard trade symbols, abbreviations and nomenclature.

Guarantees

Review the designers' listings on the next pages for specific details on their individual guarantees. You may return plans to any of the designers, within 30 days, if they are not suitable for your community's building codes. All of the designers guarantee the suitability of their designs and drawings up to the full refund of your purchase price.

Copyrights and Permission to Build

All of the plans presented in this book are protected by U.S. and international copyright law. Please don't reproduce them without the designer's permission. By purchasing a set of drawings you're securing permission to build one copy of that design. If you plan to build more than one copy of building, contact the designer for for information on additional fees.

How Many Sets of Plans Will You Need ?

To build your barn or backbuilding, you'll probably need more than one set of construction drawings. Take advantage of the discounts that the designers offer for additional prints of the same design. You'll need a set of prints for yourself, one for each contractor who bids on your building, and one or more for your bank if you're financing the project. Check with your building department to see how many review sets they require. If you live in a community or subdivision that has design criteria, you may also need to present a set to your review committee.

How to Send for Your Plans

Construction drawings and study plans for the barns and backbuildings presented in this book have been prepared and are sold by different architects and designers. Their sales policies vary. To order your copies of plans for any building, find the Design Number, the price, and the name of the designer. You'll find that information on the page in this book that has the illustration and description of your building. Then read the designer's sales policy, listed on one of the next two pages.

Mail your payment directly to the designer. Please specify the Design Number and the quantity of prints you need, and remember to include any cost of postage and handling. If you and your building's designer are in the same state, please include any necessary sales tax.

Charge Card Orders

Some of the designers can accept charge card orders. Fax your order to the number listed. Please include your address, a daytime phone number, the Design Number and quantity of the drawings you want, your credit card company (Discover Card, Visa, etc.), the exact name you use on your credit card account, and its expiration date.

Canadian Customers

Please make payment in U.S. Dollars or adjust your payment in Canadian dollars to reflect the current exchange rate. The drawings presented in this book are prepared to U.S. codes and standards and may have to be adapted by your building professional.

Design Numbers and Titles

The Design Numbers and titles used in this book are sometimes different than the ones that the designers use to label their drawings in their own catalogs and files. Don't be surprised if your drawings arrive with a different title or number.

The Designers

Donald J. Berg, AIA

P.O. Box 698, Rockville Centre, NY 11571-0698

Charge cards accepted: MasterCard, Visa

Fax charge card orders to: 516 536-4081

Please add $4.00 per order, to cover postage and handling. Prices listed are for the first set ordered of any design. Additional prints of a design, ordered at the same time, are $10.00 each. New York state residents please add sales tax. Donald J. Berg, AIA offers a moneyback guarantee on plans returned within 30 days of purchase.

Chestnut Oak Co.

3810 Old Mountain Road, West Suffield, CT 06093-2125

Study plans for Chestnut Oak Co.'s timber-framed barns are available for $15.00, postpaid. They may be returned within 30 days for a refund. Connecticut residents, please add sales tax.

Homestead Design, Inc.

P.O. Box 2010, Port Townsend, WA 98368

Charge cards accepted: MasterCard, Visa

Phone or Fax charge card orders to: 360 385-9983

Please add $4.00 per order to cover postage and handling. Prices listed are for the first set ordered of any design. Additional prints of a design are 50% of the listed price when ordered at the same time. Washington residents please add sales tax. Homestead Design, Inc. offers a moneyback guarantee on plans returned within 30 days of purchase.

Just Outbuildings

P.O. Box 42, Brewster, NY 10509-0042

Free first-class postage is include in the price of all plans. Prices listed are for the first set of construction drawings ordered. Additional sets of prints of a design are 50% of the listed price, when ordered at the same time. New York state residents, please add sales tax. Just Outbuildings offers a moneyback guarantee on plans returned within 30 days of purchase. Architect George J. Gaspar can make custom alterations to Just Outbuildings' plans. Send a sketch or complete description to Just Outbuildings for a price quote on the cost of the customizing.

McKie Roth Design, Inc.

P.O. Box 31, Castine, ME 04421

Charge cards accepted: MasterCard, Visa

Fax charge card orders to: 207 326-9513

Please add $5.00 per order to cover shipping. Prices listed are for the first set of any design. Additional sets of the same design ordered at the same time are just $10.00 per set. Maine residents, please add 6% sales tax. Drawings may be returned for a refund, within 30 days.

North Woods Joinery

P.O. Box 1166, Burlington, VT 05402-1166

Study plans for North Wood's timber-framed barns are available for $15.00 each, post-paid. They may be returned, within 30 days for a refund. Vermont residents, please add sales tax.

Russell Swinton Oatman Design Associates, Inc.

132 Mirick Road, Princeton, MA 01541

Please add $3.00 to cover the cost of postage of one set of plans or $4.50 for two or more sets. Prices listed are for the first set of construction drawings ordered. Additional sets of the same design, ordered at the same time or within 90 days, are available for $15.00 each and $20.00 for design #RO5. Massachusetts residents, please add sales tax. Plans may be returned for a refund within 30 days if they are not acceptable to your community's building officials. Architect Russell Oatman can provide custom modifications and site plans. Contact him for complete information.

Royalston Oak Timber Frames

122 North Fitzwilliam Road, Royalston, MA 01331

Study plans for Royalston Oak's timber-framed barns are available for $15.00 each post-paid. They may be returned, within 30 days for a refund. Massachusetts residents, please add sales tax.

Sheldon Design, Inc.

1330 Route 206 - #204, Skillman, NJ 08558

Charge cards accepted: Discover, MasterCard, Visa

Phone: 800 572-5934 Fax: 609 693-5976

Please add $4.00 per order to cover postage and handling. Prices listed are for the first set of drawings ordered of any design. Additional prints of a design are $15.00 each if ordered at the same time or within 30 days. New Jersey residents please add 6% sales tax. Sheldon Design, Inc. offers a moneyback guarantee on plans returned within 30 days. Architect Andy Sheldon can provide custom designs and modifications of his standard designs at a rate of approximately $1.50/sq. ft.

Stiles Designs

4 Albertine Lane, East Hampton, NY 11937

Please add $4.00 per order to cover postage and handling. Prices listed are for the first set of drawings of a design. Additional sets of the same design, ordered at the same time are just $10.00 each. New York state residents, please add sales tax. Stiles Designs will refund your purchase price on plans returned within 30 days.

Anthony Wolfe, Architect

Mail orders to: Donald J. Berg, AIA, P.O. Box 698, Rockville Centre, NY 11571

Charge cards accepted: MasterCard, Visa

Fax charge card orders to: 516 536-4081

Please add $4.00 per order, to cover postage and handling. Prices listed are for the first set ordered. Additional sets ordered at the same time are $20.00 each. New York state residents, please add sales tax. Plans may be returned within 30 days of purchase for a full refund.

*A stable design
from the book
Country Homes
by
George and F. W. Woodward,
1865*

This stable may be constructed either of wood, or of stone. It contains stalls for four horses, and affords space for their accomodation, together with a harness room and a tool closet. This latter is a convenience very essential to the comfort of the owner, as well as to the proper care and preservation of such implements as belong especially to the carriage house and stable.

This building should be surrounded and screened with fruit trees and shrubbery, and then, with its evident architectural effects, it will become an attractive feature in the landscape of which it becomes a part, with the other accessories of the elegant country home.

FEED SHOOTS

COACH R.
27X30.

TOOL C.
9'6"X10

HARNESS R.
5 6 X10 6

Plan

References & Resources
10

Yesterday's beautiful farmsteads didn't get that way by chance. Farmers prided themselves on being well read, on keeping up-to-date on building technology and on carefully planning their places. It was very common to see farmers pictured with the latest issue of a farm journal tucked into their pocket or the plan of their farmstead by their side.

On the next few pages, you'll find the best of today's guide books on specific types of backbuildings and about do-it-yourself construction methods. You'll also find sources for additional information on designing, planning, and building, on restoring barns, and on barn history. Most of the books are inexpensive and easy to find. Many will be at your local library or book shop. Some of the information is free for the asking or on the Internet.

Any of the books listed with an order number may be purchased from: Donald J. Berg, AIA, P.O. Box 698, Rockville Centre, NY 11571. Send the listed price and $2.00 per book to cover the cost of postage.

Building Codes

Your region is probably covered by one of the four major building codes. Call or write to get information or to order code books.

Building Officals & Code Administrators International (BOCA)
4051 West Flossmore Road, Country Club Hills, IL 60477
708 799-2300

Council of American Building Officials (CABO)
5203 Leesburg Pike, Falls Church, VA 22041
703 931-4533

International Conefrence of Building Officials (ICBO)
5360 South Workman Mill Road, Whittier, CA 90601
310 699-0541

Southern Building Code Congress International (SBCCI)
900 Montclair Road, Birmingham, AL 35213
205 591-1853

Building Book Catalogs

These orginizations offer free or inexpensive catalogs full of hard-to-find books on building and woodworking specialties. Call or write them for your copy.

Builder's Booksource
Free Catalog
1817 4th Street, Berkeley, CA 94710
510 845-6874

Linden Publishing
Woodworkers Library catalog: $2.00
336 West Bedford, #107, Fresno, CA 93711
209 431-4736

Lofty Branch Book Store
Free Catalog
P.O. Box 308, Canandaigua, NY 14424
800 783-6954

National Association of Home Builders Bookstore
Free Catalog
1201 15th Street, NW, Washington, DC 20005
800 368-5242

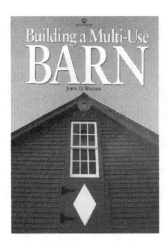 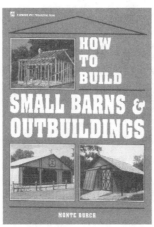 

If you're planning to build your own barn or backbuilding you'll want to study these building guides. Even if you're planning on hiring a pro to do the work, these books will help you understand and enjoy the building process and make the best design choices.

Building Small Barns, Sheds & Shelters, by Monte Burch. From permits to the finish coat of paint, this book will guide you through your building process. Burch describes the advantages of different framing methods, roof styles and materials and backs his text with useful reference tables and concise construction details. The book presents plans for five small barns, two two-box stables, a root and storm cellar, a carport, a tool shed, a woodshed, a smokehouse and shelters for hens, pigs and rabbits. 236 pages, 8 1/2 x 11, softcover, $14.95. **Order #GW03**

How to Build Small Barns & Outbuildings, by Monte Burch. In this book, Burch combines great building advice with plans for 20 small buildings. You'll find designs for 3 small all-purpose barns, an 8 stall horse barn, various animal shelters, two garages and 4 garden sheds. 280 pages, 8 1/2 x 11, softcover, $18.95. **Order #GW04**

Building a Multi-Use Barn, by John D. Wagner. Instead of presenting a variety of designs, builder John Wagner shows the versatility that's possible with one good barn. Using a 24' by 30' plan and simple framing, Wagner alters the interior layout to create a tractor garage and garden shed, a studio, a workshop and office, and a stable. His ideas should be considered by anyone looking for practical uses for old barns and heritage frames. Besides being a design guide, this book covers all the basics of light frame construction with easy-to-read text, photos and great illustrations. 221 pages, 8 1/2 x 11, softcover, $14.95. **Order #WP02**

Architects

The national office of the American Institute can direct you to your state's association. They'll provide you with names of members in your area and useful literature about architectural services. Call 202 626-7300, or write to :

The American Institute of Architects
1735 New York Ave., NW, Washington, DC 20006

Guides to Working with Stone

 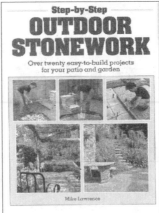 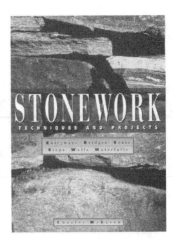

Nothing ties a building to its site like a pretty field-stone foundation. Most barn and backbuilding projects will look better and have lasting value with the addition of stone retaining walls and paving. These guidebooks will help you get great results.

Building With Stone, by Charles McRaven. A step-by-step guide to working with stone on a variety of projects, including walls, dams, bridges, a barbecue pit, a fireplace, a root cellar, a springhouse and a wellhouse. A very good section on repairing old stone walls should be of value to anyone who is restoring a heritage barn. 192 pages, 8 1/2 x 11, softcover, $17.95. **Order #GW05**

Step-by-Step Outdoor Stonework, by Mike Lawrence. Twenty different projects are presented in color photos and detailed drawings. Lawrence concentrates on patios, paving, steps, garden walls, stone furniture and decorative ponds - projects that home owners can handle themselves with this concise guide. 96 pages, 8 1/2 x 11, softcover, $18.95. **Order #GW06**

Stonework Techniques and Projects, by Charles McRaven. A guide to the basics of stone work that concentrates on the most common projects: retaining walls, stone fences, foundations and steps, and then adds a bit more for the adventuresome: a fireplace, an arched bridge, and a moon gate. A good book for the do-it-yourselfer or to learn what to look for in hiring a professional stone mason. 183 pages, 8 1/2 x 11, softcover, $18.95. **Order #GW07**

Fences

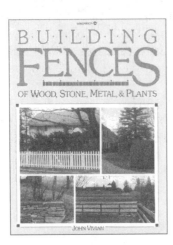

Building Fences of Wood, Stone, Metal, & Plants, by John Vivian. As the title says, this is a general primer on building all types of fences and on growing hedges. The section on stone and masonry is particularly thorough. Great illustrations by Liz Buell, straight forward text and detailed photographs of works in progress make this a good resource for both novice and experienced builders. 188 pages, 8 1/2 x 11, softcover, $13.95. **Order #WP03**

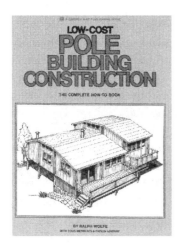 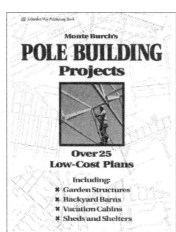 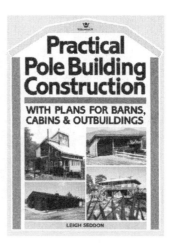

Pole building is the easiest way to build, the second time you do it. If you're not depending on an experienced pole building contractor for your project, you'll need to read these guide books:

Practical Pole Building Construction, by Leigh Seddon. A complete builders' guide with reference tables, over 100 clear illustrations, photos and building plans for a lean-to animal shelter, a two horse stable, a combination two car garage and woodshed, and more. 176 pages, 8 1/2" x 11", softcover, $10.95. **Order #WP01**

Pole Building Projects, by Monte Burch. This book presents the basics of pole building and design and includes plans you can build for barns, sheds, garden structures and garages. Useful tables, charts, photos and illustrations form a step by step guide. 208 pages, 8 1/2" x 11", softcover, $17.95. **Order #GW01**

Low Cost Pole Construction, by Ralph Wolfe, with Doug Merrilees and Evelyn Loveday. The classic guide is still a valuable introduction to the basics and history of pole building. It includes 290 photographs and illustrations and building plans for garages, small barns, a storage shed and a woodshed. 182 pages, 8 1/2" x 11", softcover, $14.95. **Order #GW02**

One of the best overall reference books on pole-framing, is the *Post-Frame Building Handbook: Materials, Design Considerations, Construction Procedures.* "Post-framing" is the term preferred by engineers, but it's not as widely used as "pole-framing." Regardless, the book is an authoritative primer on design and construction with engineering formulas, details, information on regional climatic conditions, design standards, reference tables and information on construction procedures. This book is invaluable to pole-frame builders and designers. It's available directly from the publisher:

Northeast Regional Agricultural Engineering Service (NRAES)
Cooperative Extension, 152 Riley-Robb Hall, Ithaca, NY 14853-5701
Phone 607 255-7654 for current pricing or for a free copy of their publications catalog.

Shed Building

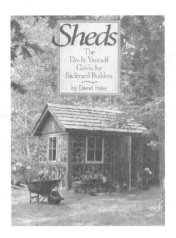

Sheds: The Do-it-Yourself Guide for Backyard Builders, by David Stiles. This book has the information you need to design and build your own ideal backyard shed. In fact, it serves as a great primer for any construction project. It covers planning, designing, permits, materials and construction methods. Stiles will guide you through the process, step-by-step, from the paper plan to hanging up your tools - in the shed you built! There are hundreds of great illustrations and projects you can try: a Victorian garden shed, cupolas, a Japanese boat shed, trash and recycling sheds, woodsheds, a pool pavilion and many more. 142 pages, 8 1/2 x 11, softcover, $17.95. **Order #FF01**

Timber Framing

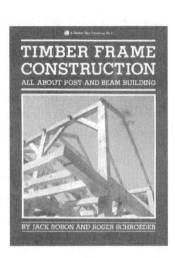

Timber Frame Construction: All About Post-and-Beam Building, by Jack Sobon and Roger Schroeder. This book presents a great history lesson on timber framing and explains the basics of today's methods of post-and-beam construction. Jack Sobon is one of the pioneers of the American revival of the ancient craft. Few can tell the story as well. 204 pages, 8 1/2 x 11, softcover, $18.95. **Order #GW08**

Timber Framing Magazines

Joiners' Quarterly is the journal of timber framing and traditional building methods. It features colorful, illustrated articles on natural and sustainable building systems. It's aimed at professional builders and designers, but anyone who loves traditional buildings will enjoy each issue. Subscriptions are $22.00 for one year. Write to:

Joiners' Quarterly
P.O. Box 249, Brownfield, ME 04010

Timber Framing is the quarterly journal published by the Timber Framers Guild of North America. Every issue brings authoritative articles on history, design, construction and engineering. Subscribe for an annual rate of $20.00 by writing to:

TFGNA
P.O. Box 1075, Bellingham, WA 98227

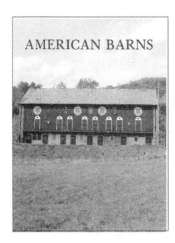  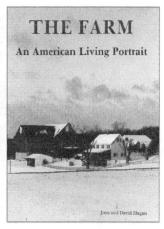

American Barns, by Stanley Schuler. Take a tour of 240 old and new barns throughout the United States with this book's clear photographs and concise descriptions. You'll have a good introduction to our regional styles and to the amazing variety of different barn types. If you're planning to design or build a barn, you can't help but be inspired by the many photos of building details. 224 pages, 8 1/2 x 11, softcover, $29.95. **Order #SB01**

American Country Building Design: Rediscovered Plans for 19th Century Farmhouses, Cottages, Landscapes, Barns, Carriage Houses & Outbuildings, by Donald J. Berg, AIA. Yesterday's best designs are shown in original engravings, plans and in the words of their designers. Historic woodwork details and site planning techniques can help you design and build in the American country tradition. 160 pages, 8 1/2 x 11, softcover, $14.95. **Order #SP01**

The Farm: an American Living Portrait, by Joan and David Hagan. Hundreds of color photographs document the American family farm and its passing way of life. Crisp shots and close-up details of beautiful barns, outbuildings and cupolas are sure to inspire your building project. 160 color pages, 8 1/2 x 11, softcover, $29.95. **Order #SB02**

Visit an old farmstead to get inspiration on your new building project. Bring a camera to record nice details. Farms across the country are being preserved and restored and are open to the public. To find information about sites near you, refer to the *Farm Museum Directory: A Guide Through America's Farm Past*. You can order the 64 page, softcover book directly from the publisher for just $5.50, postpaid. Send to:

Stemgas Publishing Company
P.O. Box 328, Lancaster, PA 17608

The *Farm Museum Directory* was published in cooperation with **The Association for Living Historical Farms and Agricultural Museums, Inc.** ALFHAM has over 1,000 members throughout the world who work at preserving our rural heritage and bringing history to life for us. Your membership can support their efforts and provide you with information about farm and living history museums in your area. For a free brochure, write to:

ALHFAM c/o Judith M. Sheridan, Secretary-Treasurer
Brownwood Farm, 877 Route 45 NW, North Bloomfield, OH 44450

Photo of an Amish community's barn raising, courtesy of Charles Leik, The Barn Journal

On-Line Resources

It's pretty amazing, but the best source for information about traditional barn raisings is the Internet. Two on-line magazines offer schedules of events, reviews of books and forums for the exchange of ideas on the preservation of historic methods and on preserving barns themselves.

The Barn Journal, is a website dedicated to the appreciation and preservation of traditional farm architecture. Editor Charles Liek reviews new publications and posts news about events and resources. People are invited to share ideas, and they do! Many of the manufacturers and craftsmen listed in *Barn & Backbuildings'* Directory were suggested by the good folks who visit *The Barn Journal.* The free classified ads are a terrific way to buy and sell old barns or frames and to find authentic hardware and fittings. Check it out at: http://museum.cl.msu.edu/barn.

Barn Again! is a website run by *Successfull Farming Magazine* and The National Trust for Historic Preservation. It provides information to help owners of historic barns rehabilitate them and put them back to productive use. Even if you're not restoring a barn, you'll find useful publications and great advice from staff experts and contributors. One recent query was "why red?". To find out, log on at: htpp://www.agriculture.com/contents/ba!/ba!.html.

Index

Barns & Backbuildings'
Bigger Book Building Bee

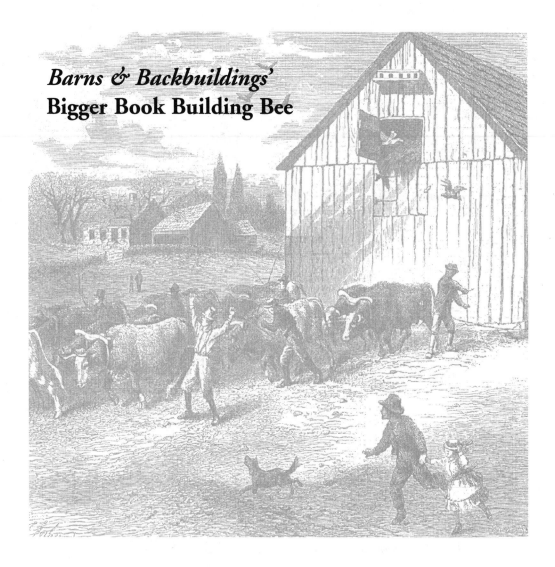

The next edition of *Barns and Backbuildings* needs your help. Like yesterday's barn raising and moving bees, the more folks like you who lend a hand, the better it will be. If you know of manufacturers, publishers, building guide books, plans, designers, restoration experts, kit builders, timber framers or artisans who should be featured in the book or listed in the Directory, please let us know. If you've purchased a great backyard product or gotten great service, let us know that too. We'll pass your news on to thousands of readers.

If you're the first to suggest a name, you'll receive a free copy of the next edition as soon as it's off the press. Fax your ideas and your name and address to: 516 536-4081, or mail them to:

Barns & Backbuildings
c/o Don Berg
P.O. Box 698, Rockville Centre, NY 11571-0698